LITERARY TOUCHSTONE CLASSICS

P.O. Box 658 Clayton, Delaware 19938 • www.prestwickhouse.com

Senior Editor: Paul Moliken

Editor: Darlene Gilmore

Cover Design: Larry Knox & Jen Mendoza

Production: Jen Mendoza

Prestwick House
LITERARY TOUCHSTONE CLASSICS™

P.O. Box 658 • Clayton, Delaware 19938
Tel: 1.800.932.4593
Fax: 1.888.718.9333
Web: www.prestwickhouse.com

ISBN 978-1-58049-220-1

STRATEGIES

STRATEGIES

Strategies for Understanding Shakespeare's Language

1. When reading verse, note the appropriate phrasing and intonation.

   DO NOT PAUSE AT THE END OF A LINE unless there is a mark of punctuation. Shakespearean verse has a rhythm of its own, and once a reader gets used to it, the rhythm becomes very natural to speak in and read. Beginning readers often find it helpful to read a short pause at a comma and a long pause for a period, colon, semicolon, dash, or question mark.
   Here's an example from *The Merchant of Venice*, Act IV, Scene i:

   > The quality of mercy is not strain'd, (*short pause*)
   > It droppeth as the gentle rain from heaven
   > Upon the place beneath: (*long pause*) it is twice blest; (*long pause*)
   > It blesseth him that gives, (*short pause*) and him that takes; (*long pause*)
   > 'Tis mightiest in the mighties; (*long pause*) it becomes
   > The throned monarch better than his crown; (*long pause*)

2. Read from punctuation mark to punctuation mark for meaning.

   In addition to helping you read aloud, punctuation marks define units of thought. Try to understand each unit as you read, keeping in mind that periods, colons, semicolons, and question marks signal the end of a thought. Here's an example from *The Taming of the Shrew*, Act I, Scene i:

   > LUC. Tranio, I saw her coral lips to move,
   > And with her breath she did perfume the air;
   > Sacred, and sweet, was all I saw in her.
   > TRA. Nay, then, 'tis time to stir him from his trance.
   > I pray, awake, sir: if you love the maid,
   > Bend thoughts and wits to achieve her.

   The first unit of thought is from "Tranio" to "air":

CONTENTS

He saw her lips move, and her breath perfumed the air.

The second thought ("Sacred, and sweet…") re-emphasizes the first.

Tranio replies that Lucentio needs to awaken from his trance and try to win "the maid." These two sentences can be considered one unit of thought.

3. In an **inverted sentence**, the verb comes before the subject. Some lines will be easier to understand if you put the subject first and reword the sentence. For example, look at the line below:

   "*Never was seen so black a day as this:*" (*Romeo and Juliet*, Act IV, Scene v)

   You can change its inverted pattern so it is more easily understood:

   "*A day as black as this was never seen:*"

4. An **ellipsis** occurs when a word or phrase is left out. In *Romeo and Juliet*, Benvolio asks Romeo's father and mother if they know the problem that is bothering their son. Romeo's father answers:

   "*I neither know* **it** *nor can learn of* **him**" (*Romeo and Juliet*, Act I, Scene i)

   This sentence can easily be understood to mean,

   "*I neither know [the cause of] it,*
   nor can [I] learn [about it from] him."

5. As you read longer speeches, keep track of the subject, verb, and object—who did what to whom.

   In the clauses below, note the subject, verbs, and objects:

   ROSS: The king hath happily received, Macbeth,
   The news of thy success: and when he reads
   Thy personal venture in the rebel's fight… (*Macbeth*, Act I, Scene iii)

   1st clause: *The king hath happily received, Macbeth,/The news of thy success:*
   SUBJECT – The king
   VERB – has received
   OBJECT – the news [of Macbeth's success]

2nd clause: *and when he reads/thy personal venture in the rebel's fight,*
SUBJECT – he [the king]
VERB – reads
OBJECT – [about] your venture

In addition to following the subject, verb, and object of a clause, you also need to track pronoun references. In the following soliloquy, Romeo, who is madly in love with Juliet, secretly observes her as she steps out on her balcony. To help you keep track of the pronoun references, we've made margin notes. (Note that the feminine pronoun sometimes refers to Juliet, but sometimes does not.)

> But, soft! what light through yonder window breaks?
> It is the east, and Juliet is the sun!
> Arise, fair sun, and kill the envious moon,
> Who* is already sick and pale with grief, — *"Who" refers to the moon.*
> That thou her* maid* art more fair than she:* — *"thou her maid" refers to Juliet, the sun.* *"she" and "her" refer to the moon.*

In tracking the line of action in a passage, it is useful to identify the main thoughts that are being expressed and paraphrase them. Note the following passage in which Hamlet expresses his feelings about the death of his father and the remarriage of his mother:

> O God! a beast that wants discourse of reason
> Would have mourn'd longer—married with my uncle,
> My father's brother, but no more like my father
> Than I to Hercules. (*Hamlet*, Act I, Scene ii)

Paraphrasing the three main points, we find that Hamlet is saying:

- a mindless beast would have mourned the death of its mate longer than my mother did
- she married my uncle, my father's brother
- my uncle is not at all like my father

If you are having trouble understanding Shakespeare, the first rule is to read it out loud, just as an actor rehearsing would have to do. That will help you understand how one thought is connected to another.

6. Shakespeare frequently uses **metaphor** to illustrate an idea in a unique way. Pay careful attention to the two dissimilar objects or ideas being compared.

In *Macbeth*, Duncan, the king says:

> I have begun to plant thee, and will labour
> To make thee full of growing. (*Macbeth*, Act I, Scene v)

The king compares Macbeth to a tree he can plant and watch grow.

7. An **allusion** is a reference to some event, person, place, or artistic work, not directly explained or discussed by the writer; it relies on the reader's familiarity with the item referred to. Allusion is a quick way of conveying information or presenting an image. In the following lines, Romeo alludes to Diana, goddess of the hunt and of chastity, and to Cupid's arrow (love).

> ROMEO: Well, in that hit you miss: she'll not be hit
> with Cupid's arrow, she hath Dian's wit;
> and in strong proof of chastity well arm'd
> (*Romeo and Juliet*, Act I, Scene i)

8. Contracted words are words in which a letter has been left out. Some that frequently appear:

be't	on't	wi'	do't
t'	'sblood	'gainst	ta'en
i'	'tis	e'en	'bout
know'st	'twill	ne'er	o'
o'er			

9. Archaic, obsolete, and familiar words with unfamiliar definitions may also cause problems.

   - **Archaic Words**: Some archaic words, like *thee*, *thou*, *thy*, and *thine*, are instantly understandable, while others, like *betwixt*, cause a momentary pause.

   - **Obsolete Words**: If it were not for the notes in a Shakespeare text, obsolete words could be a problem; words like *beteem* are usually not found in student dictionaries. In these situations, however, a quick glance at the book's notes will solve the problem.

   - **Familiar Words with Unfamiliar Definitions**: Another problem is those familiar words whose definitions have changed. Because readers think they know the word, they do not check the notes. For example, in this comment from *Much Ado About Nothing*, Act I, Scene i, the word *an* means "if":

BEATRICE: Scratching could not make it worse, *an* 'twere such a face as yours were.

For this kind of word, we have included margin notes.

10. Wordplay—puns, double entendres, and malapropisms:

    - A **pun** is a literary device that achieves humor or emphasis by playing on ambiguities. Two distinct meanings are suggested either by the same word or by two similar-sounding words.

    - A **double entendre** is a kind of pun in which a word or phrase has a second, usually sexual, meaning.

    - A **malapropism** occurs when a character mistakenly uses a word that he or she has confused with another word. In *Romeo and Juliet*, the Nurse tells Romeo that she needs to have a "confidence" with him, when she should have said "conference." Mockingly, Benvolio then says she probably will "indite" (rather than "invite") Romeo to dinner.

READING POINTERS

Reading Pointers for Sharper Insights

To better appreciate Shakespeare's *Twelfth Night*, consider the following points:

Setting:

Twelfth Night takes place during the Christian celebration of Epiphany, which occurs on January 6th, the twelfth night after Christmas. The holiday celebrates the visit of the wise men to the infant Jesus, symbolizing Christ's divinity to the world. During Elizabethan times, the celebration consisted of feasts, gift-giving, and general merry-making. Most importantly, however, the Epiphany celebration was marked by a reversal of the normal order of things. There were masquerades, role reversals, and a general sense of things being turned upside down. This spirit of lighthearted insanity and foolishness is a central element of the play.

Thematic Concepts:

- love as a form of insanity
- love as suffering or illness
- the uncertainty of identity
- the uncertainty of gender
- the folly of prideful ambition
- the fickle nature of love
- the fleeting nature of youth and beauty
- the comic and tragic effects of deception
- the idea that events are controlled by fate

Symbols and Motifs:

- the darkness of Malvolio's prison
- Olivia's gifts to Cesario
- disguises and altered identities
- songs and poems
- courtship and romantic speeches
- nautical references and sailing metaphors
- hunting references and metaphors
- references to Greek and Roman mythology
- puns and wordplay
- sexual innuendoes and vulgar jokes
- the satirizing of philosophers and intellectuals

Historical Context:

William Shakespeare wrote *Twelfth Night* in England in 1601.

- Queen Elizabeth (1533-1603) ruled England from 1558 to 1603.
- The English Renaissance was at its height, with great achievements in the areas of literature, philosophy, religion, science, music, and theatre.
- The Protestant Reformation, the movement to break away from the established doctrines of the Roman Catholic Church, continued to change the religious lives of Europeans.
- England enjoyed a time of expansion and exploration, creating new trade routes and making frequent visits to North and South America.
- England adhered to a system of social classes, ranging from nobility to middle class to poor.

Twelfth Night
or, What You Will

By William Shakespeare

Dramatis Personæ

ORSINO, Duke of Illyria.
SEBASTIAN, a young Gentleman, brother to Viola.
ANTONIO, a Sea Captain, friend to Sebastian.
A SEA CAPTAIN, friend to Viola.
VALENTINE, Gentleman attending on the Duke.
CURIO, Gentleman attending on the Duke.
SIR TOBY BELCH, Uncle to Olivia.
SIR ANDREW AGUECHEEK.
MALVOLIO, Steward to Olivia.
FABIAN, Servant to Olivia.
FESTE, CLOWN, Servant to Olivia.
OLIVIA, a rich Countess.
VIOLA, in love with the Duke.
MARIA, Olivia's Woman.
LORDS,
PRIESTS,
SAILORS,
OFFICERS,
MUSICIANS,
and other ATTENDANTS.

SCENE: *A City in Illyria; and the Sea-coast near it.*

ACT I

Twelfth Night or, What You Will

ACT I

SCENE I
Duke Orsino's Palace.

[Enter Duke, Curio, Lords; Musicians attending.]

DUKE ORSINO: If music be the food of love, play on;
Give me excess of it, that, surfeiting,
The appetite may sicken, and so die.†
That strain[1] again! it had a dying fall:[2]
5 O, it came o'er my ear like the sweet sound,
That breathes upon a bank of violets,
Stealing and giving odour! Enough; no more;
'Tis not so sweet now as it was before.
O spirit of love! how quick and fresh art thou,
10 That, notwithstanding thy capacity
Receiveth as the sea, nought[3] enters there,
Of what validity and pitch[4] soe'er,[5]
But falls into abatement and low price,[6]†
Even in a minute: so full of shapes is fancy
15 That it alone is high fantastical.†
CURIO: Will you go hunt, my lord?
DUKE ORSINO: What, Curio?
CURIO: The hart.[7]
DUKE ORSINO: Why, so I do, the noblest that I have:†
20 O, when mine eyes did see Olivia first,
Methought she purg'd the air of pestilence!
That instant was I turn'd into a hart;
And my desires, like fell[8] and cruel hounds,
E'er since pursue me.†

[1]*musical note*
[2]*cadence*
[3]*nothing*
[4]*height*
[5]*soever (as in whatsoever)*
[6]*diminished value*
[7]*deer*
[8]*fierce*

†Terms marked in the text with (†) can be looked up in the Glossary for additional information.

[Enter Valentine.]

25 How now! what news from her?

Valentine: So please my lord, I might not be admitted;
But from her handmaid do return this answer:
The element[9] itself, till seven years' heat,†
Shall not behold her face at ample view;
30 But, like a cloistress, she will veiled walk
And water once a day her chamber round
With eye-offending brine:† all this to season
A brother's dead love, which she would keep fresh
And lasting in her sad remembrance.
35 Duke Orsino: O, she that hath a heart of that fine frame
To pay this debt of love but to a brother,
How will she love, when the rich golden shaft†
Hath kill'd the flock of all affections else
That live in her; when liver, brain, and heart,†
40 These sovereign thrones, are all supplied, and fill'd
Her sweet perfections with one self king!
Away before me to sweet beds of flowers:
Love-thoughts lie rich when canopied with bowers.

[Exeunt.]

[9] *sky, air*

SCENE II
The sea-coast.

[Enter Viola, Captain, and Sailors.]

Viola: What country, friends, is this?
Captain: This is Illyria,† lady.
Viola: And what should I do in Illyria?
My brother he is in Elysium.†
5 Perchance he is not drown'd: what think you, sailors?
Captain: It is perchance that you yourself were saved.
Viola: O my poor brother! and so perchance may he be.
Captain: True, madam; and, to comfort you with chance,
Assure yourself, after our ship did split,
10 When you and those poor number saved with you
Hung on our driving boat, I saw your brother,
Most provident in peril, bind himself,

Courage and hope both teaching him the practice,
To a strong mast that lived upon the sea;
15 Where, like Arion on the dolphin's back,†
I saw him hold acquaintance with the waves
So long as I could see.

VIOLA: For saying so, there's gold.
Mine own escape unfoldeth to my hope,
20 Whereto thy speech serves for authority,
The like of him. Know'st thou this country?

CAPTAIN: Ay, madam, well; for I was bred and born
Not three hours' travel from this very place.

VIOLA: Who governs here?

25 CAPTAIN: A noble duke, in nature
As in name.

VIOLA: What is his name?

CAPTAIN: Orsino.

VIOLA: Orsino! I have heard my father name him.
30 He was a bachelor then.

CAPTAIN: And so is now, or was so very late;
For but a month ago I went from hence,[1]
And then 'twas fresh in murmur,[2] —as, you know,
What great ones do the less will prattle of,—
35 That he did seek the love of fair Olivia.

VIOLA: What's she?

CAPTAIN: A virtuous maid, the daughter of a count
That died some twelvemonth since; then leaving her
In the protection of his son, her brother,
40 Who shortly also died: for whose dear love,
They say, she hath abjured the company
And sight of men.

VIOLA: O that I served that lady
And might not be delivered to the world,
45 Till I had made mine own occasion mellow,
What my estate is!†

CAPTAIN: That were hard to compass;[3]
Because she will admit no kind of suit,[4]
No, not the Duke's.

50 VIOLA: There is a fair behavior in thee, captain;
And though that nature with a beauteous wall
Doth oft close in pollution,† yet of thee
I will believe thou hast a mind that suits
With this thy fair and outward character.

[1] *from this place*

[2] *it was rumored*

[3] *That will be hard to achieve*

[4] *request or petition*

[5] I beg you

55 I prithee,[5] and I'll pay thee bounteously,
Conceal me what I am, and be my aid
For such disguise as haply shall become
The form of my intent.† I'll serve this duke:
Thou shalt present me as an eunuch† to him:
60 It may be worth thy pains; for I can sing
And speak to him in many sorts of music
That will allow me very worth his service.
What else may hap[6] to time I will commit;
Only shape thou silence to my wit.[7]

[6] happen
[7] cleverness

65 CAPTAIN: Be you his eunuch, and your mute I'll be:
When my tongue blabs, then let mine eyes not see.
VIOLA: I thank thee: lead me on. *[Exeunt.]*

SCENE III
Olivia's House.

[Enter Sir Toby Belch† and Maria.]

SIR TOBY: What a plague means my niece, to take the death of her brother thus? I am sure care's an enemy to life.

MARIA: By my troth,[1] Sir Toby, you must come in earlier o' nights: your cousin,† my lady, takes great exceptions to
5 your ill hours.

[1] Truly

SIR TOBY: Why, let her except, before excepted.†

MARIA: Ay, but you must confine yourself within the modest limits of order.

SIR TOBY: Confine? I'll confine myself no finer than I am:
10 these clothes are good enough to drink in; and so be these boots too: an[2] they be not, let them hang themselves in their own straps.

[2] if

MARIA: That quaffing and drinking will undo you: I heard my lady talk of it yesterday; and of a foolish knight that you
15 brought in one night here to be her wooer.[3]

[3] suitor

SIR TOBY: Who, Sir Andrew Aguecheek?†

MARIA: Ay, he.

SIR TOBY: He's as tall a man as any's in Illyria.

MARIA: What's that to the purpose?

20 SIR TOBY: Why, he has three thousand ducats† a year.

MARIA: Ay, but he'll have but a year in all these ducats: he's a very fool, and a prodigal.

SIR TOBY: Fie,[4] that you'll say so! he plays o' the viol-de-gamboys,† and speaks three or four languages word for word
25 without book, and hath all the good gifts of nature.

MARIA: He hath indeed, almost natural:† for besides that he's a fool, he's a great quarreler; and but that he hath the gift of a coward to allay the gust[5] he hath in quarrelling, 'tis thought among the prudent he would quickly have the gift
30 of a grave.

SIR TOBY: By this hand, they are scoundrels and substractors[6] that say so of him. Who are they?

MARIA: They that add, moreover, he's drunk nightly in your company.

35 SIR TOBY: With drinking healths to my niece: I'll drink to her as long as there is a passage in my throat and drink in Illyria. He's a coward and a coystrill[7] that will not drink to my niece till his brains turn o' the toe like a parish-top.† What, wench! Castiliano vulgo!† for here comes Sir Andrew Agueface.

[Enter Sir Andrew Aguecheek.]

40 SIR ANDREW: Sir Toby Belch! how now, Sir Toby Belch!

SIR TOBY: Sweet Sir Andrew!

SIR ANDREW: Bless you, fair shrew.

MARIA: And you too, sir.

SIR TOBY: Accost,[8] Sir Andrew, accost.

45 SIR ANDREW: What's that?

SIR TOBY: My niece's chambermaid.

SIR ANDREW: Good Mistress Accost,† I desire better acquaintance.

MARIA: My name is Mary, sir.

50 SIR ANDREW: Good Mistress Mary Accost,—

SIR TOBY: You mistake, knight; 'accost' is front[9] her, board[10] her, woo her, assail[11] her.

SIR ANDREW: By my troth, I would not undertake her in this company. Is that the meaning of 'accost'?

55 MARIA: Fare you well, gentlemen.

SIR TOBY: An thou let part so, Sir Andrew, would thou mightst never draw sword again.

SIR ANDREW: An you part so, mistress, I would I might never draw sword again. Fair lady, do you think you have fools
60 in hand?

MARIA: Sir, I have not you by the hand.

[4]*an expression of contempt or distaste*

[5]*taste or appetite*

[6]*slanderers*

[7]*someone inferior or of low birth; a mean person*

[8]*Approach and greet*

[9]*face*

[10]*greet*

[11]*seduce*

[12] Indeed

SIR ANDREW: Marry,[12] but you shall have; and here's my hand.

MARIA: Now, sir, thought is free. I pray you, bring your hand
65 to the buttery-bar† and let it drink.

[13] Why

SIR ANDREW: Wherefore,[13] sweetheart? what's your metaphor?

MARIA: It's dry, sir.†

SIR ANDREW: Why, I think so: I am not such an ass but I can
70 keep my hand dry. But what's your jest?

MARIA: A dry jest, sir.

SIR ANDREW: Are you full of them?

MARIA: Ay, sir, I have them at my fingers' ends: marry, now I let go your hand, I am barren. *[Exit Maria.]*

75 SIR TOBY: O knight, thou lackest a cup of canary:† when did I see thee so put down?

SIR ANDREW: Never in your life, I think; unless you see canary put me down. Methinks sometimes I have no more wit than a Christian or an ordinary man has; but I am great
80 eater of beef, and I believe that does harm to my wit.†

SIR TOBY: No question.

SIR ANDREW: An I thought that, I'd forswear it. I'll ride home tomorrow, Sir Toby.

SIR TOBY: *Pourquoi*,[14] my dear knight?

[14] *[French]* Why

[15] languages

85 SIR ANDREW: What is 'Pourquoi'? Do or not do? I would I had bestowed that time in the tongues[15] that I have in fencing, dancing, and bear-baiting.† Oh, had I but followed the arts!

SIR TOBY: Then hadst thou had an excellent head of hair.

90 SIR ANDREW: Why, would that have mended my hair?

SIR TOBY: Past question; for thou seest it will not curl by nature.

SIR ANDREW: But it becomes me well enough, does't not?

SIR TOBY: Excellent; it hangs like flax on a distaff; and I hope
95 to see a housewife take thee between her legs and spin it off.†

[16] Truly

[17] nearby

[18] rank in society

[19] wealth

SIR ANDREW: Faith,[16] I'll home tomorrow, Sir Toby: your niece will not be seen; or, if she be, it's four to one she'll none of me. The Count himself here hard by[17] woos her.

100 SIR TOBY: She'll none o' the Count: she'll not match above her degree,[18] neither in estate,[19] years, nor wit; I have heard her swear't. Tut, there's life in't, man.

SIR ANDREW: I'll stay a month longer. I am a fellow o' the

strangest mind i' the world; I delight in masques[20] and revels
105 sometimes altogether.

SIR TOBY: Art thou good at these kickshawses,[21] knight?

SIR ANDREW: As any man in Illyria, whatsoever he be, under the degree of my betters; and yet I will not compare with an old man.

110 SIR TOBY: What is thy excellence in a galliard,[22] knight?

SIR ANDREW: Faith, I can cut a caper.[23]

SIR TOBY: And I can cut the mutton to't.†

SIR ANDREW: And, I think I have the back-trick simply as strong as any man in Illyria.

115 SIR TOBY: Wherefore are these things hid? wherefore have these gifts a curtain before 'em? are they like to take dust, like Mistress Mall's† picture? why dost thou not go to church in a galliard and come home in a coranto[24]? My very walk should be a jig; I would not so much as make water but in
120 a sink-a-pace.† What dost thou mean? Is it a world to hide virtues in? I did think, by the excellent constitution of thy leg, it was formed under the star of a galliard.

SIR ANDREW: Ay, 'tis strong, and it does indifferent well in flame-colour'd stock.[25] Shall we set about some revels?

125 SIR TOBY: What shall we do else? were we not born under Taurus?

SIR ANDREW: Taurus? that's sides and heart.†

SIR TOBY: No, sir; it is legs and thighs. Let me see thee caper; ha! higher! ha, ha! excellent!

[Exeunt.]

[20]*masquerades*

[21]*trifles*

[22]*a type of lively dance*

[23]*a type of dance*

[24]*a type of running dance*

[25]*stocking*

SCENE IV
Duke Orsino's Palace.

[Enter Valentine, and Viola in man's attire.]

VALENTINE: If the Duke continue these favours towards you, Cesario, you are like to be much advanced: he hath known you but three days, and already you are no stranger.

VIOLA: You either fear his humour[1] or my negligence, that you
5 call in question the continuance of his love: is he inconstant, sir, in his favours?

VALENTINE: No, believe me.

VIOLA: I thank you. Here comes the Count.

[1]*temper, attitude*

[Enter Duke, Curio, and Attendants.]

Duke Orsino: Who saw Cesario, ho?
10 **Viola**: On your attendance, my lord; here.
Duke Orsino: Stand you awhile aloof.—Cesario,
Thou know'st no less but all; I have unclasp'd
To thee the book even of my secret soul:
Therefore, good youth, address thy gait[2] unto her;
15 Be not denied access, stand at her doors,
And tell them, there thy fixed foot shall grow
Till thou have audience.
Viola: Sure, my noble lord,
If she be so abandon'd to her sorrow
20 As it is spoke, she never will admit me.
Duke Orsino: Be clamorous and leap all civil bounds,
Rather than make unprofited return.
Viola: Say I do speak with her, my lord, what then?
Duke Orsino: O, then unfold the passion of my love,
25 Surprise her with discourse of my dear faith:
It shall become thee well to act my woes;
She will attend it better in thy youth
Than in a nuncio's[3] of more grave aspect.[4]
Viola: I think not so, my lord.
30 **Duke Orsino**: Dear lad, believe it;
For they shall yet belie thy happy years,
That say thou art a man: Diana's lip†
Is not more smooth and rubious;[5] thy small pipe[6]
Is as the maiden's organ, shrill and sound,
35 And all is semblative[7] a woman's part.
I know thy constellation[8]† is right apt
For this affair. Some four or five attend him:
All, if you will; for I myself am best
When least in company. Prosper well in this,
40 And thou shalt live as freely as thy lord,
To call his fortunes thine.
Viola: I'll do my best
To woo your lady. *[Aside]* Yet, a barful strife![9]
Whoe'er I woo, myself would be his wife.†

[Exeunt.]

[2]*direct your steps*

[3]*messenger's*

[4]*appearance*

[5]*bright red*

[6]*throat*

[7]*resembles*

[8]*nature, character*

[9]*a difficult situation filled with obstacles*

SCENE V
Olivia's House.

[Enter Maria and Clown.]

MARIA: Nay, either tell me where thou hast been, or I will not open my lips so wide as a bristle may enter in way of thy excuse: my lady will hang thee for thy absence.

CLOWN: Let her hang me: he that is well hanged in this world
5 needs to fear no colours.†

MARIA: Make that good.

CLOWN: He shall see none to fear.

MARIA: A good lenten[1] answer: I can tell thee where that saying was born, of, 'I fear no colours.'

10 CLOWN: Where, good Mistress Mary?

MARIA: In the wars;† and that may you be bold to say in your foolery.

CLOWN: Well, God give them wisdom that have it; and those that are fools, let them use their talents.†

15 MARIA: Yet you will be hanged for being so long absent; or, to be turned away, is not that as good as a hanging to you?

CLOWN: Many a good hanging prevents a bad marriage; and, for turning away, let summer bear it out.†

MARIA: You are resolute, then?

20 CLOWN: Not so, neither; but I am resolved on two points.

MARIA: That if one break, the other will hold; or, if both break, your gaskins[2] fall.†

CLOWN: Apt, in good faith; very apt. Well, go thy way; if Sir Toby would leave drinking, thou wert as witty a piece of Eve's
25 flesh as any in Illyria.†

MARIA: Peace, you rogue; no more o' that; here comes my lady: make your excuse wisely; you were best. *[Exit.]*

CLOWN: Wit, an't be thy will, put me into good fooling!† Those wits that think they have thee, do very oft prove fools; and I,
30 that am sure I lack thee, may pass for a wise man: for what says Quinapalus?† 'Better a witty fool than a foolish wit.'

[Enter Olivia and Malvolio.]

God bless thee, lady!

OLIVIA: Take the fool away.

CLOWN: Do you not hear, fellows? Take away the lady.

[1]*thin, sparse*

[2]*trousers*

[3]barren, empty

[4]my lady

[5]mender of clothing

[6]commanded

[7]instruct in a question and answer format

[8]doesn't he improve?

35 OLIVIA: Go to, you're a dry[3] fool; I'll no more of you: besides, you grow dishonest.

CLOWN: Two faults, madonna,[4] that drink and good counsel will amend: for give the dry fool drink, then is the fool not dry; bid the dishonest man mend himself: if he mend,
40 he is no longer dishonest; if he cannot, let the botcher[5] mend him. Any thing that's mended is but patched. Virtue that transgresses is but patched with sin; and sin that amends is but patched with virtue.† If that this simple syllogism will serve, so; if it will not, what rem-
45 edy? As there is no true cuckold but calamity, so beauty's a flower:† The lady bade[6] take away the fool; therefore, I say again, take her away.

OLIVIA: Sir, I bade them take away you.

CLOWN: Misprision in the highest degree! Lady, '*Cucullus*
50 *non facit monachum*'—that's as much to say as I wear not motley in my brain.† Good madonna, give me leave to prove you a fool.

OLIVIA: Can you do it?

CLOWN: Dexteriously, good madonna.

55 OLIVIA: Make your proof.

CLOWN: I must catechize[7] you for it, madonna. Good my mouse of virtue,† answer me.

OLIVIA: Well, sir, for want of other idleness, I'll 'bide your proof.

60 CLOWN: Good madonna, why mourn'st thou?

OLIVIA: Good fool, for my brother's death.

CLOWN: I think his soul is in hell, madonna.

OLIVIA: I know his soul is in heaven, fool.

CLOWN: The more fool, madonna, to mourn for your brother's
65 soul being in heaven. Take away the fool, gentlemen.

OLIVIA: What think you of this fool, Malvolio?† Doth he not mend?[8]

MALVOLIO: Yes; and shall do till the pangs of death shake him. Infirmity, that decays the wise, doth ever make the
70 better fool.

CLOWN: God send you, sir, a speedy infirmity, for the better increasing your folly! Sir Toby will be sworn that I am no fox; but he will not pass his word for two pence that you are no fool.

75 OLIVIA: How say you to that, Malvolio?

MALVOLIO: I marvel your ladyship takes delight in such a

barren[9] rascal; I saw him put down the other day with an ordinary fool that has no more brain than a stone. Look you now, he's out of his guard already; unless you laugh and min-
80 ister occasion[10] to him, he is gagged. I protest, I take these wise men that crow so at these set kind of fools, no better than the fools' zanies.†

OLIVIA: O, you are sick of[11] self-love, Malvolio,† and taste with a distempered appetite. To be generous, guiltless, and of free
85 disposition, is to take those things for bird-bolts that you deem cannon-bullets. There is no slander in an allowed fool, though he do nothing but rail; nor no railing in a known discreet man, though he do nothing but reprove.†

CLOWN: Now Mercury endue thee with leasing,† for thou speak-
90 est well of fools!

[Re-enter Maria.]

MARIA: Madam, there is at the gate a young gentleman much desires to speak with you.

OLIVIA: From the Count Orsino, is it?

MARIA: I know not, madam; 'tis a fair young man, and well
95 attended.

OLIVIA: Who of my people hold him in delay?

MARIA: Sir Toby, madam, your kinsman.[12]

OLIVIA: Fetch him off,[13] I pray you; he speaks nothing but madman. Fie on him! *[Exit Maria]*
100 Go you, Malvolio: if it be a suit[14] from the Count, I am sick, or not at home; what you will[15] to dismiss it.
[Exit Malvolio.]
Now you see, sir, how your fooling grows old, and people dislike it.

CLOWN: Thou hast spoke for us, madonna, as if thy eldest
105 son should be a fool; whose skull Jove† cram with brains, for,—here he comes,—one of thy kin, has a most weak *pia mater*.†

[Enter Sir Toby.]

OLIVIA: By mine honour, half drunk. What is he at the gate, cousin?

110 SIR TOBY: A gentleman.

OLIVIA: A gentleman? What gentleman?

[9] *empty of wit*

[10] *give opportunity*

[11] *with*

[12] *relative*

[13] *Get rid of him*

[14] *message of courtship*

[15] *do whatever you must*

[16] fool, idiot

SIR TOBY: 'Tis a gentleman here—a plague o' these pickle-herring!†—How now, sot?[16]

CLOWN: Good Sir Toby!

115 OLIVIA: Cousin, cousin, how have you come so early by this lethargy?

SIR TOBY: Lechery! I defy lechery.† There's one at the gate.

OLIVIA: Ay, marry; what is he?

SIR TOBY: Let him be the devil an he will, I care not: give me
120 faith, say I. Well, it's all one.† *[Exit.]*

OLIVIA: What's a drunken man like, fool?

CLOWN: Like a drowned man, a fool, and a madman: one draught above heat† makes him a fool; the second mads him; and a third drowns him.

[17] coroner

[18] conduct an investigation regarding my cousin

125 OLIVIA: Go thou and seek the crowner,[17] and let him sit o' my coz;[18] for he's in the third degree of drink; he's drowned: go, look after him.

CLOWN: He is but mad yet, madonna; and the fool shall look to the madman. *[Exit.]*

[Re-enter Malvolio.]

130 MALVOLIO: Madam, yond young fellow swears he will speak with you. I told him you were sick; he takes on him to understand so much, and therefore comes to speak with you. I told him you were asleep; he seems to have a foreknowledge of that too, and therefore comes to speak with
135 you. What is to be said to him, lady? he's fortified against any denial.

OLIVIA: Tell him, he shall not speak with me.

MALVOLIO: Has been told so; and he says, he'll stand at your door like a sheriff's post,† and be the supporter to a
140 bench, but he'll speak with you.

OLIVIA: What kind of man is he?

MALVOLIO: Why, of mankind.

OLIVIA: What manner of man?

MALVOLIO: Of very ill manner; he'll speak with you, will you
145 or no.

[19] appearance

OLIVIA: Of what personage[19] and years is he?

MALVOLIO: Not yet old enough for a man, nor young enough for a boy; as a squash is before 'tis a peascod, or a codling, when 'tis almost an apple: 'tis with him in standing water,

150 between boy and man.† He is very well-favoured,[20] and he speaks very shrewishly;[21] one would think his mother's milk were scarce out of him.

OLIVIA: Let him approach. Call in my gentlewoman.

MALVOLIO: Gentlewoman, my lady calls. *[Exit.]*

[Re-enter Maria.]

155 OLIVIA: Give me my veil; come, throw it o'er my face. We'll once more hear Orsino's embassy.[22]

[Enter Viola.]

VIOLA: The honourable lady of the house, which is she?

OLIVIA: Speak to me; I shall answer for her. Your will?

VIOLA: Most radiant, exquisite, and unmatchable beauty,—I pray
160 you, tell me if this be the lady of the house, for I never saw her: I would be loath[23] to cast away my speech, for besides that it is excellently well penned, I have taken great pains to con[24] it. Good beauties, let me sustain no scorn; I am very comptible,[25] even to the least sinister usage.

165 OLIVIA: Whence[26] came you, sir?

VIOLA: I can say little more than I have studied, and that question's out of my part. Good gentle one, give me modest assurance, if you be the lady of the house, that I may proceed in my speech.

170 OLIVIA: Are you a comedian?

VIOLA: No, my profound heart: and yet, by the very fangs of malice I swear, I am not that I play. Are you the lady of the house?

OLIVIA: If I do not usurp myself, I am.

175 VIOLA: Most certain, if you are she, you do usurp yourself; for what is yours to bestow is not yours to reserve.† But this is from my commission:[27] I will on with my speech in your praise, and then show you the heart of my message.

OLIVIA: Come to what is important in't: I forgive you the
180 praise.

VIOLA: Alas, I took great pains to study it, and 'tis poetical.

OLIVIA: It is the more like to be feigned: I pray you, keep it in. I heard you were saucy[28] at my gates, and allowed your approach rather to wonder at you than to hear you. If you

[20] *good-looking*

[21] *tartly; in a quarrelsome way*

[22] *message*

[23] *I would be unwilling*

[24] *memorize, learn*

[25] *sensitive*

[26] *From where*

[27] *mandate, order*

[28] *disrespectful, rude*

185 be not mad, be gone; if you have reason, be brief: 'tis not that time of moon with me to make one in so skipping a dialogue.†

MARIA: Will you hoist sail, sir? here lies your way.†

VIOLA: No, good swabber; I am to hull here a little longer.
190 Some mollification for your giant, sweet lady.†

OLIVIA: Tell me your mind.

VIOLA: I am a messenger.†

OLIVIA: Sure, you have some hideous matter to deliver, when the courtesy of it is so fearful. Speak your office.[29]

195 VIOLA: It alone concerns your ear. I bring no overture of war, no taxation of homage: I hold the olive in my hand; my words are as full of peace as matter.†

OLIVIA: Yet you began rudely. What are you? what would you?

200 VIOLA: The rudeness that hath appeared in me have I learned from my entertainment. What I am, and what I would, are as secret as maidenhead;[30] to your ears, divinity; to any other's, profanation.[31]

OLIVIA: Give us the place alone: we will hear this divinity.

[Exit Maria.]

205 Now, sir, what is your text?[32]

VIOLA: Most sweet lady,—

OLIVIA: A comfortable doctrine, and much may be said of it. Where lies your text?

VIOLA: In Orsino's bosom.

210 OLIVIA: In his bosom? In what chapter of his bosom?

VIOLA: To answer by the method, in the first[33] of his heart.

OLIVIA: O, I have read it: it is heresy. Have you no more to say?

VIOLA: Good madam, let me see your face.

215 OLIVIA: Have you any commission from your lord to negotiate with my face? you are now out of your text:[34] but we will draw the curtain and show you the picture.

[Unveiling.]

Look you, sir, such a one I was this present. Is't not well
220 done?†

VIOLA: Excellently done, if God did all.

OLIVIA: 'Tis in grain,† sir; 'twill endure wind and weather.

VIOLA: 'Tis beauty truly blent,[35] whose red and white
Nature's own sweet and cunning hand laid on:
225 Lady, you are the cruell'st she alive,

[29] *business*

[30] *chastity, virginity*

[31] *profanity*

[32] *written message*

[33] *first chapter*

[34] *off your official subject*

[35] *blended*

If you will lead these graces to the grave
And leave the world no copy.†

OLIVIA: O, sir, I will not be so hard-hearted; I will give out divers[36] schedules of my beauty: it shall be inventoried,
230 and every particle and utensil labelled to my will: as, item, two lips, indifferent red; item, two grey eyes, with lids to them; item, one neck, one chin, and so forth. Were you sent hither[37] to praise me?

VIOLA: I see you what you are: you are too proud;
235 But, if you were the devil, you are fair.
My lord and master loves you: O, such love
Could be but recompensed,[38] though you were crown'd
The nonpareil of beauty!

OLIVIA: How does he love me?

240 VIOLA: With adorations, fertile tears,
With groans that thunder love, with sighs of fire.

OLIVIA: Your lord does know my mind; I cannot love him:
Yet I suppose him virtuous, know him noble,
Of great estate, of fresh and stainless youth;
245 In voices well divulged,[39] free, learn'd, and valiant,
And in dimension[40] and the shape of nature,
A gracious person: but yet I cannot love him;
He might have took his answer long ago.

VIOLA: If I did love you in my master's flame,
250 With such a suffering, such a deadly life,
In your denial I would find no sense;
I would not understand it.

OLIVIA: Why, what would you?

VIOLA: Make me a willow cabin at your gate,†
255 And call upon my soul within the house;
Write loyal cantons[41] of contemned[42] love
And sing them loud, even in the dead of night;
Halloo[43] your name to the reverberate hills
And make the babbling gossip of the air
260 Cry out 'Olivia!' O, you should not rest
Between the elements of air and earth,
But you should pity me.

OLIVIA: You might do much.
What is your parentage?[44]

265 VIOLA: Above my fortunes, yet my state is well:
I am a gentleman.

OLIVIA: Get you to your lord;

[36] *various*
[37] *here*
[38] *repaid*
[39] *spoken*
[40] *size and shape*
[41] *songs*
[42] *condemned*
[43] *Call out*
[44] *heritage, origin*

I cannot love him: let him send no more;
Unless, perchance, you come to me again,
270 To tell me how he takes it. Fare you well:
I thank you for your pains: spend this for me.†

VIOLA: I am no fee'd post,[45] lady; keep your purse:
My master, not myself, lacks recompense.
Love make his heart of flint that you shall love;
275 And let your fervor, like my master's, be
Placed in contempt!† Farewell, fair cruelty. *[Exit.]*

OLIVIA: 'What is your parentage?'
'Above my fortunes, yet my state is well:
I am a gentleman.' I'll be sworn thou art;
280 Thy tongue, thy face, thy limbs, actions, and spirit,
Do give thee five-fold blazon: not too fast: soft, soft![46]
Unless the master were the man.† How now?
Even so quickly may one catch the plague?
Methinks I feel this youth's perfections
285 With an invisible and subtle stealth
To creep in at mine eyes.† Well, let it be.
What, ho, Malvolio!

[Re-enter Malvolio.]

MALVOLIO: Here, madam, at your service.

OLIVIA: Run after that same peevish messenger,
290 The County's man: he left this ring behind him,†
Would I or not: tell him I'll none of it.
Desire him not to flatter with his lord,
Nor hold him up with hopes; I am not for him:
If that the youth will come this way tomorrow,
295 I'll give him reasons for't: hie[47] thee, Malvolio.

MALVOLIO: Madam, I will. *[Exit.]*

OLIVIA: I do I know not what, and fear to find
Mine eye too great a flatterer for my mind.
Fate, show thy force: ourselves we do not owe;
300 What is decreed must be, and be this so.† *[Exit.]*

[45] *paid messenger*

[46] *hush; be still*

[47] *hurry*

ACT II

SCENE I
The sea-coast.

[Enter Antonio and Sebastian.]

ANTONIO: Will you stay no longer, nor will you not that I go with you?

SEBASTIAN: By your patience,[1] no. My stars shine darkly over me: the malignancy of my fate might perhaps distemper yours;[2]† therefore I shall crave of you your leave that I may bear my evils alone: it were a bad recompense for your love, to lay any of them on you.

ANTONIO: Let me know of you whither[3] you are bound.

SEBASTIAN: No, sooth,[4] sir: my determinate voyage is mere extravagancy.[5] But I perceive in you so excellent a touch of modesty, that you will not extort from me what I am willing to keep in; therefore it charges me in manners[6] the rather to express myself. You must know of me then, Antonio, my name is Sebastian, which I called Rodorigo. My father was that Sebastian of Messaline, whom I know you have heard of. He left behind him myself and a sister, both born in an hour: if the heavens had been pleased, would we had so ended!† but you, sir, altered that; for some hours before you took me from the breach[7] of the sea was my sister drowned.

ANTONIO: Alas the day!

SEBASTIAN: A lady, sir, though it was said she much resembled me, was yet of many accounted[8] beautiful: but, though I could not with such estimable[9] wonder overfar[10] believe that, yet thus far I will boldly publish[11] her; she bore a mind that envy could not but call fair. She is drowned already, sir, with salt water, though I seem to drown her remembrance again with more.

[1] *allowance*

[2] *put you in a bad mood*

[3] *where*

[4] *truly*

[5] *vagrancy*

[6] *I am required to show good manners*

[7] *breaking waves*

[8] *considered*

[9] *admiring*

[10] *too far*

[11] *declare publicly*

[12]for the lack of hospitality I have shown you

[13]for being the cause of your trouble

[14]may cry

[15]recreation, amusement

ANTONIO: Pardon me, sir, your bad entertainment.[12]

SEBASTIAN: O good Antonio, forgive me your trouble.[13]

30 ANTONIO: If you will not murder me for my love, let me be your servant.†

SEBASTIAN: If you will not undo what you have done—that is, kill him whom you have recovered—desire it not. Fare ye well at once: my bosom is full of kindness, and I
35 am yet so near the manners of my mother, that upon the least occasion more mine eyes will tell tales of me.[14] I am bound to the Count Orsino's court: farewell. *[Exit.]*

ANTONIO: The gentleness of all the gods go with thee!
I have many enemies in Orsino's court,
40 Else would I very shortly see thee there.
But, come what may, I do adore thee so,
That danger shall seem sport,[15] and I will go.

[Exit.]

SCENE II
A street.

[Enter Viola; Malvolio following.]

[1]just now

[2]here

[3]bold, daring

[4]appearance

MALVOLIO: Were you not even now[1] with the Countess Olivia?

VIOLA: Even now, sir; on a moderate pace I have since arrived but hither.[2]

5 MALVOLIO: She returns this ring to you, sir: you might have saved me my pains, to have taken it away yourself. She adds, moreover, that you should put your lord into a desperate assurance she will none of him: and one thing more, that you be never so hardy[3] to come again in his
10 affairs, unless it be to report your lord's taking of this. Receive it so.

VIOLA: She took the ring of me: I'll none of it.†

MALVOLIO: Come, sir, you peevishly threw it to her; and her will is, it should be so returned: if it be worth stooping
15 for, there it lies in your eye; if not, be it his that finds it. *[Exit.]*

VIOLA: I left no ring with her: what means this lady?
Fortune forbid my outside[4] have not charm'd her!

She made good view of me; indeed, so much,
That sure methought her eyes had lost her tongue,
20 For she did speak in starts distractedly.
She loves me, sure; the cunning of her passion
Invites me in this churlish messenger.
None of my lord's ring! why, he sent her none.
I am the man: if it be so, as 'tis,
25 Poor lady, she were better[5] love a dream.
Disguise, I see, thou art a wickedness,
Wherein the pregnant[6] enemy does much.
How easy is it for the proper-false[7]
In women's waxen[8] hearts to set their forms![9]†
30 Alas, our frailty is the cause, not we!
For such as we are made of, such we be.
How will this fadge?[10] my master loves her dearly;
And I, poor monster, fond as much on him;
And she, mistaken, seems to dote on me.
35 What will become of this? As[11] I am man,
My state is desperate for my master's love;
As I am woman,—now alas the day!—
What thriftless sighs shall poor Olivia breathe!
O time! thou must untangle this, not I;
40 It is too hard a knot for me to untie!† *[Exit.]*

[5] *would be better off to*

[6] *expert, clever*

[7] *deceivers*

[8] *made of wax, therefore easily manipulated*

[9] *impressions, shapes*

[10] *turn out*

[11] *If*

SCENE III
Olivia's house.

[Enter Sir Toby and Sir Andrew.]

SIR TOBY: Approach, Sir Andrew: not to be abed after midnight is to be up betimes;[1] and 'diluculo surgere,'† thou know'st.

SIR ANDREW: Nay; by my troth,[2] I know not: but I know, to be up late is to be up late.

5 SIR TOBY: A false conclusion: I hate it as an unfilled can.[3] To be up after midnight and to go to bed then, is early: so that to go to bed after midnight is to go to bed betimes. Do not our lives consist of the four elements?†

SIR ANDREW: Faith, so they say; but I think it rather consists of
10 eating and drinking.

SIR TOBY: Thou'rt a scholar; let us therefore eat and drink. Marian, I say! a stoup[4] of wine!

[1] *early*

[2] *truly*

[3] *empty drinking cup*

[4] *cup, drinking vessel*

[Enter Clown.]

SIR ANDREW: Here comes the fool, i' faith.

CLOWN: How now, my hearts.[5] Did you never see the picture of 'we three'?†

SIR TOBY: Welcome, ass.[6] Now let's have a catch.[7]

SIR ANDREW: By my troth, the fool has an excellent breast.[8] I had rather than forty shillings I had such a leg, and so sweet a breath to sing, as the fool has. In sooth, thou wast in very gracious fooling last night, when thou spokest of Pigrogromitus, of the Vapians passing the equinoctial of Queubus;† 'twas very good, i' faith. I sent thee sixpence for thy leman:[9] hadst it?[10]

CLOWN: I did impeticos thy gratillity; for Malvolio's nose is no whipstock: my lady has a white hand, and the Myrmidons are no bottle-ale houses.†

SIR ANDREW: Excellent! why, this is the best fooling, when all is done. Now, a song.

SIR TOBY: Come on; there is sixpence for you: let's have a song.

SIR ANDREW: There's a testril[11] of me too: if one knight give a—

CLOWN: Would you have a love-song, or a song of good life?

SIR TOBY: A love-song, a love-song.

SIR ANDREW: Ay, ay: I care not for good life.

CLOWN: [sings]

O, mistress mine, where are you roaming?
O, stay and hear; your true love's coming,
That can sing both high and low:
Trip no further, pretty sweeting;
Journeys end in lovers meeting,
Every wise man's son doth know.

SIR ANDREW: Excellent good, i' faith.

SIR TOBY: Good, good.

CLOWN:

What is love? 'tis not hereafter;
Present mirth hath present laughter;
What's to come is still unsure:
In delay there lies no plenty;
Then come kiss me, sweet and twenty,
Youth's a stuff will not endure.

[5] dear ones

[6] idiot

[7] song sung in the manner of a round

[8] singing ability

[9] lover, sweetheart

[10] have you received it?

[11] sixpence (a unit of money)

SIR ANDREW: A mellifluous voice, as I am true knight.
SIR TOBY: A contagious breath.
SIR ANDREW: Very sweet and contagious, i' faith.
55 SIR TOBY: To hear by the nose, it is dulcet in contagion.[12] But shall we make the welkin[13] dance indeed? Shall we rouse the night-owl in a catch that will draw three souls out of one weaver?† shall we do that?
SIR ANDREW: An you love me, let's do't: I am dog[14] at a catch.
60 CLOWN: By'r lady,[15] sir, and some dogs will catch well.
SIR ANDREW: Most certain. Let our catch be, 'Thou knave.'
CLOWN: 'Hold thy peace, thou knave' knight? I shall be constrained in't to call thee knave, knight.
SIR ANDREW: 'Tis not the first time I have constrained one to call
65 me knave. Begin, fool; it begins 'Hold thy peace.'
CLOWN: I shall never begin if I hold my peace.
SIR ANDREW: Good, i' faith! Come, begin. *[They sing a catch.]*

[Enter Maria.]

MARIA: What a caterwauling do you keep here! If my lady have not called up her steward Malvolio and bid him turn you out
70 of doors, never trust me.
SIR TOBY: My lady's a Cataian, we are politicians; Malvolio's a Peg-a-Ramsey, and *[Singing.]* 'Three merry men be we.'† Am not I consanguineous?[16] am I not of her blood? Tillyvalley,[17] Lady! *[sings]* 'There dwelt a man in Babylon, lady, lady.'†
75 CLOWN: Beshrew me,[18] the knight's in admirable fooling.
SIR ANDREW: Ay, he does well enough if he be disposed, and so do I too; he does it with a better grace, but I do it more natural.
SIR TOBY: *[Sings]* 'O, the twelfth day of December,'—
80 MARIA: For the love o' God, peace!

[Enter Malvolio.]

MALVOLIO: My masters, are you mad? or what are you? Have ye no wit, manners, nor honesty, but to gabble like tinkers[19] at this time of night? Do ye make an alehouse of my lady's house, that ye squeak out your coziers'[20] catches without
85 any mitigation or remorse of voice? Is there no respect of place, persons, nor time in you?
SIR TOBY: We did keep time, sir, in our catches. Sneck up![21]

[12] *sweet sounding to the point of sickness*

[13] *sky*

[14] *expert, well-versed*

[15] *By our lady (meaning the Virgin Mary)*

[16] *of the same blood*

[17] *Nonsense*

[18] *Curse me*

[19] *menders of broken objects (used derogatorily)*

[20] *cobblers*

[21] *an exclamation which literally means "go get hanged"*

MALVOLIO: Sir Toby, I must be round[22] with you. My lady bade me tell you, that, though she harbours you as her kinsman, she's nothing allied to your disorders. If you can separate yourself and your misdemeanors, you are welcome to the house; if not, an it would please you to take leave of her, she is very willing to bid you farewell. (90)

SIR TOBY: 'Farewell, dear heart, since I must needs be gone.'†

MARIA: Nay, good Sir Toby. (95)

CLOWN: 'His eyes do show his days are almost done.'

MALVOLIO: Is't even so?

SIR TOBY: 'But I will never die.'

CLOWN: Sir Toby, there you lie.[23]

MALVOLIO: This is much credit to you. (100)

SIR TOBY: 'Shall I bid him go?'

CLOWN: 'What an if you do?'

SIR TOBY: 'Shall I bid him go, and spare not?'

CLOWN: 'O, no, no, no, no, you dare not.'

SIR TOBY: Out o' tune, sir: ye lie. Art any more than a steward?[24] Dost thou think, because thou art virtuous, there shall be no more cakes and ale?† (105)

CLOWN: Yes, by Saint Anne, and ginger shall be hot i' the mouth† too.

SIR TOBY: Thou'rt i' the right. Go, sir, rub your chain with crumbs.† A stoup of wine, Maria! (110)

MALVOLIO: Mistress Mary, if you prized my lady's favour at anything more than contempt, you would not give means[25] for this uncivil rule:[26] she shall know of it, by this hand.[27] *[Exit.]* (115)

MARIA: Go shake your ears.†

SIR ANDREW: 'Twere as good a deed as to drink when a man's a-hungry, to challenge him the field,[28] and then to break promise with him and make a fool of him.

SIR TOBY: Do't, knight; I'll write thee a challenge: or I'll deliver thy indignation to him by word of mouth. (120)

MARIA: Sweet Sir Toby, be patient for tonight: since the youth of the Count's was today with thy lady, she is much out of quiet.[29] For Monsieur Malvolio, let me alone with him: if I do not gull[30] him into a nayword,[31] and make him a common recreation,[32] do not think I have wit enough to lie straight in my bed: I know I can do it. (125)

SIR TOBY: Possess us,[33] possess us; tell us something of him.

MARIA: Marry, sir, sometimes he is a kind of Puritan.†

[22] *plain, honest*

[23] *you are lying*

[24] *a household manager*

[25] *resources, opportunities*

[26] *disorderly conduct*

[27] *a mild oath, like "I pledge"*

[28] *challenge him to a duel*

[29] *agitated*

[30] *trick*

[31] *slogan, byword, example*

[32] *amusement*

[33] *Inform us*

130 SIR ANDREW: O, if I thought that I'd beat him like a dog.

SIR TOBY: What, for being a puritan? thy exquisite reason, dear knight?

SIR ANDREW: I have no exquisite reason for't, but I have reason good enough.

135 MARIA: The devil a Puritan that he is, or anything constantly, but a time-pleaser;[34] an affectioned ass that cons state[35] without book and utters it by great swarths:[36] the best persuaded of himself, so crammed, as he thinks, with excellencies, that it is his grounds of faith that all that look on him love him;
140 and on that vice in him will my revenge find notable cause to work.

SIR TOBY: What wilt thou do?

MARIA: I will drop in his way some obscure epistles of love; wherein, by the colour of his beard, the shape of his leg,
145 the manner of his gait, the expressure[37] of his eye, forehead, and complexion, he shall find himself most feelingly personated.[38] I can write very like my lady, your niece; on a forgotten matter we can hardly make distinction of our hands.[39]

SIR TOBY: Excellent! I smell a device.[40]

150 SIR ANDREW: I have't in my nose too.

SIR TOBY: He shall think, by the letters that thou wilt drop, that they come from my niece, and that she is in love with him.

MARIA: My purpose is, indeed, a horse of that colour.[41]

SIR ANDREW: And your horse now would make him an ass.

155 MARIA: Ass, I doubt not.

SIR ANDREW: O 'twill be admirable!

MARIA: Sport royal,[42] I warrant you: I know my physic[43] will work with him. I will plant you two, and let the fool make a third, where he shall find the letter:† observe his construc-
160 tion[44] of it. For this night, to bed, and dream on the event. Farewell. *[Exit.]*

SIR TOBY: Good night, Penthesilea.†

SIR ANDREW: Before me,[45] she's a good wench.

SIR TOBY: She's a beagle true-bred, and one that adores me: what
165 o' that?

SIR ANDREW: I was adored once too.

SIR TOBY: Let's to bed, knight. Thou hadst need send for more money.

SIR ANDREW: If I cannot recover[46] your niece, I am a foul way
170 out.[47]

[34] *flatterer; one who changes positions to please everyone*

[35] *learns by heart how to appear dignified*

[36] *swaths; long strips*

[37] *expression*

[38] *represented*

[39] *writing, signature*

[40] *plan, scheme*

[41] *something similar to that*

[42] *Magnificent amusement*

[43] *medicine, cure*

[44] *interpretation*

[45] *By my soul; I swear*

[46] *win, gain*

[47] *out of money*

Sir Toby: Send for money, knight; if thou hast her not i' the end, call me cut.†

Sir Andrew: If I do not, never trust me, take it how you
175 will.

Sir Toby: Come, come; I'll go burn some sack;[48] 'tis too late to go to bed now: come, knight; come, knight.

[48] *warm up some wine*

[Exeunt.]

SCENE IV
Duke Orsino's palace.

[Enter Duke, Viola, Curio, and others.]

Duke Orsino: Give me some music. Now, good morrow,[1] friends.
Now, good Cesario, but that piece of song,
That old and antique song we heard last night:
5 Methought it did relieve my passion much,
More than light airs and recollected[2] terms
Of these most brisk and giddy-paced times:
Come, but one verse.

[1] *morning*

[2] *learned, studied*

Curio: He is not here, so please your lordship that should
10 sing it.

Duke Orsino: Who was it?

Curio: Feste, the jester, my lord; a fool that the Lady Olivia's father took much delight in. He is about the house.

Duke Orsino: Seek him out, and play the tune the while.

[Exit Curio: Music plays.]

15 Come hither, boy: if ever thou shalt love,
In the sweet pangs of it remember me;
For such as I am all true lovers are,
Unstaid[3] and skittish[4] in all motions else,
Save in the constant image of the creature
20 That is beloved. How dost thou like this tune?

[3] *volatile, changeable*

[4] *fickle*

Viola: It gives a very echo to the seat
Where Love is throned.

Duke Orsino: Thou dost speak masterly:
My life upon't,[5] young though thou art, thine eye
25 Hath stay'd[6] upon some favour[7] that it loves:
Hath it not, boy?

[5] *I would swear my life upon it*

[6] *settled*

[7] *face*

VIOLA: A little, by your favour.†
DUKE ORSINO: What kind of woman is't?
VIOLA: Of your complexion.
30 DUKE ORSINO: She is not worth thee, then. What years, i' faith?
VIOLA: About your years, my lord.
DUKE ORSINO: Too old by heaven: let still the woman take
An elder than herself: so wears she to him,
So sways she level in her husband's heart:
35 For, boy, however we do praise ourselves,
Our fancies are more giddy and unfirm,
More longing, wavering, sooner lost and worn,
Than women's are.†
VIOLA: I think it well, my lord.
40 DUKE ORSINO: Then let thy love be younger than thyself,
Or thy affection cannot hold the bent;[8]
For women are as roses, whose fair flower
Being once display'd, doth fall that very hour.
VIOLA: And so they are: alas, that they are so;
45 To die, even when they to perfection grow!

[Re-enter Curio and Clown.]

DUKE ORSINO: O, fellow, come, the song we had last night.
Mark it,[9] Cesario; it is old and plain;
The spinsters and the knitters in the sun,
And the free maids that weave their thread with bones
50 Do use to chant it: it is silly sooth,[10]
And dallies[11] with the innocence of love
Like the old age.[12]
CLOWN: Are you ready, sir?
DUKE ORSINO: Ay; prithee, sing. *[Music]*
55 CLOWN: *[Sings]*

Come away, come away, death,
And in sad cypress† let me be laid;
Fly away, fly away breath;
I am slain by a fair cruel maid.
60 My shroud of white, stuck all with yew,†
O, prepare it!
My part of death, no one so true
Did share it.

[8]*keep the tension*

[9]*Pay attention*

[10]*plain truth*

[11]*plays*

[12]*old times*

Not a flower, not a flower sweet
65 On my black coffin let there be strown;[13]
Not a friend, not a friend greet
My poor corpse, where my bones shall be thrown:
A thousand thousand sighs to save,
Lay me, O, where
70 Sad true lover never find my grave,
To weep there!

[13] strewn, scattered

DUKE ORSINO: *[giving money]* There's for thy pains.
CLOWN: No pains, sir: I take pleasure in singing, sir.
DUKE ORSINO: I'll pay thy pleasure, then.
75 CLOWN: Truly, sir, and pleasure will be paid one time or another.
DUKE ORSINO: Give me now leave to leave thee.
CLOWN: Now the melancholy god protect thee; and the tailor make thy doublet[14] of changeable taffeta,[15] for thy mind
80 is a very opal.† I would have men of such constancy[16] put to sea, that their business might be everything, and their intent everywhere; for that's it that always makes a good voyage of nothing. Farewell. *[Exit Clown.]*

[14] *a vest-like garment*

[15] *a type of silk cloth*

[16] *faithfulness*

DUKE ORSINO: Let all the rest give place.[17]
[Exeunt Curio and Attendants.]
85 Once more, Cesario,
Get thee to yond same sovereign cruelty:
Tell her, my love, more noble than the world,
Prizes not quantity of dirty lands;
The parts that fortune hath bestow'd upon her,
90 Tell her, I hold as giddily as fortune;
But 'tis that miracle and queen of gems
That nature pranks[18] her in attracts my soul.

[17] *leave*

[18] *dresses, adorns*

VIOLA: But if she cannot love you, sir?
DUKE ORSINO: I cannot be so answer'd.
95 VIOLA: Sooth, but you must.
Say that some lady, as perhaps there is,
Hath for your love as great a pang of heart
As you have for Olivia: you cannot love her;
You tell her so; must she not then be answer'd?
100 DUKE ORSINO: There is no woman's sides
Can bide the beating of so strong a passion
As love doth give my heart; no woman's heart

So big, to hold so much; they lack retention.
Alas, their love may be call'd appetite,
105 No motion of the liver, but the palate,[19]
That suffer surfeit, cloyment[20] and revolt;
But mine is all as hungry as the sea,
And can digest as much: make no compare
Between that love a woman can bear me
110 And that I owe Olivia.†

VIOLA: Ay, but I know—

DUKE ORSINO: What dost thou know?

VIOLA: Too well what love women to men may owe:
In faith, they are as true of heart as we.
115 My father had a daughter loved a man,
As it might be, perhaps, were I a woman,
I should your lordship.†

DUKE ORSINO: And what's her history?

VIOLA: A blank, my lord. She never told her love,
120 But let concealment, like a worm i' the bud,[21]
Feed on her damask cheek: she pined in thought,
And with a green and yellow melancholy
She sat like patience on a monument,
Smiling at grief.† Was not this love, indeed?
125 We men may say more, swear more: but indeed,
Our shows are more than will; for still we prove
Much in our vows, but little in our love.

DUKE ORSINO: But died thy sister of her love, my boy?

VIOLA: I am all the daughters of my father's house,
130 And all the brothers too: and yet I know not.
Sir, shall I to[22] this lady?

DUKE ORSINO: Ay, that's the theme.[23]
To her in haste: give her this jewel; say,
My love can give no place,[24] bide no denay.[25] *[Exeunt.]*

[19]*the part of the mouth responsible for tasting*

[20]*fullness to excess*

[21]*in the bud of a flower*

[22]*go to*

[23]*idea*

[24]*cannot yield or give way*

[25]*denial*

SCENE V
Olivia's garden.

[Enter Sir Toby, Sir Andrew, and Fabian.]

SIR TOBY: Come thy ways,[1] Signior Fabian.

FABIAN: Nay, I'll come: if I lose a scruple[2] of this sport, let me be boiled to death with melancholy.

[1]*Come along*

[2]*a tiny bit*

Sir Toby: Wouldst thou not be glad to have the niggardly rascally sheep-biter[3] come by some notable shame? 5

Fabian: I would exult, man: you know, he brought me out o' favour with my lady about a bear-baiting here.

Sir Toby: To anger him we'll have the bear again; and we will fool him black and blue: shall we not, Sir Andrew?

10 Sir Andrew: An we do not, it is pity of our lives.

Sir Toby: Here comes the little villain.

[Enter Maria.]

How now, my nettle of India?†

Maria: Get ye all three into the box-tree: Malvolio's coming down this walk: he has been yonder i' the sun practising behavior to his own shadow this half hour: observe him, 15 for the love of mockery; for I know this letter will make a contemplative idiot of him. Close,[4] in the name of jesting! *[The men hide themselves.]* Lie thou there; *[Throws down a letter.]* for here comes the trout that must be caught with tickling.† 20 *[Exit.]*

[Enter Malvolio.]

Malvolio: 'Tis but fortune; all is fortune. Maria once told me she did affect[5] me: and I have heard herself come thus near,[6] that, should she fancy, it should be one of my complexion.[7] Besides, she uses me with a more exalted respect than any one else that follows her. What should 25 I think on't?

Sir Toby: Here's an overweening[8] rogue!

Fabian: O, peace! Contemplation makes a rare turkey-cock of him: how he jets[9] under his advanced[10] plumes!†

30 Sir Andrew: 'Slight,[11] I could so beat the rogue!

Sir Toby: Peace, I say.

Malvolio: To be Count Malvolio!†

Sir Toby: Ah, rogue!

Sir Andrew: Pistol him,[12] pistol him.

35 Sir Toby: Peace, peace!

Malvolio: There is example for't; the lady of the Strachy married the yeoman of the wardrobe.[13]†

Sir Andrew: Fie on him, Jezebel!†

Fabian: O, peace! now he's deeply in: look how imagination blows[14] him. 40

[3] *malicious person*

[4] *Hide*

[5] *love*

[6] *come near to saying*

[7] *personality*

[8] *arrogant*

[9] *struts*

[10] *raised*

[11] *By God's light*

[12] *Shoot him*

[13] *the servant in charge of a family's clothing and linen*

[14] *inflates him*

MALVOLIO: Having been three months married to her, sitting in my state,[15]—

SIR TOBY: O, for a stone-bow[16] to hit him in the eye!

MALVOLIO: Calling my officers about me, in my branched[17] velvet gown; having come from a day-bed, where I have left Olivia sleeping. 45

SIR TOBY: Fire and brimstone!

FABIAN: O, peace, peace.

MALVOLIO: And then to have the humour of state;[18] and after a demure travel of regard,[19] telling them I know my place as I would they should do theirs, to ask for my kinsman Toby,— 50

SIR TOBY: Bolts and shackles!

FABIAN: O, peace, peace, peace! now, now.

55 MALVOLIO: Seven of my people, with an obedient start, make out for him: I frown the while; and perchance, wind up my watch, or play with my—some rich jewel. Toby approaches; courtesies[20] there to me,—

SIR TOBY: Shall this fellow live?

60 FABIAN: Though our silence be drawn from us with cars,† yet peace.[21]

MALVOLIO: I extend my hand to him thus, quenching my familiar smile with an austere regard of control,—

SIR TOBY: And does not Toby take you a blow o' the lips[22] then? 65

MALVOLIO: Saying 'Cousin Toby, my fortunes having cast me on your niece give me this prerogative of speech,'—

SIR TOBY: What, what?

MALVOLIO: 'You must amend your drunkenness.'

70 SIR TOBY: Out, scab!

FABIAN: Nay, patience, or we break the sinews of our plot.

MALVOLIO: 'Besides, you waste the treasure of your time with a foolish knight,'—

SIR ANDREW: That's me, I warrant you.

75 MALVOLIO: 'One Sir Andrew,'—

SIR ANDREW: I knew 'twas I; for many do call me fool.

MALVOLIO: What employment[23] have we here?

[Taking up the letter.]

FABIAN: Now is the woodcock near the gin.[24]

SIR TOBY: O, peace! and the spirit of humours[25] intimate[26] reading aloud to him! 80

MALVOLIO: By my life, this is my lady's hand: these be her very

[15] *dignity*

[16] *slingshot*

[17] *decorated with twig-like designs*

[18] *the disposition of authority*

[19] *round of observations*

[20] *bows*

[21] *still we remain quiet*

[22] *punch in the mouth*

[23] *business*

[24] *bird near the trap*

[25] *merriment*

[26] *suggest*

C's, her U's, and her T's; and thus makes she her great P's.†
It is, in contempt of question, her hand.

SIR ANDREW: Her C's, her U's, and her T's: why that?

85 MALVOLIO: *[Reads]* 'To the unknown beloved, this, and my good wishes:'—her very phrases! By your leave, wax. Soft! and the impressure[27] her Lucrece, with which she uses to seal:† 'tis my lady. To whom should this be?

[27]*stamp*

FABIAN: This wins him, liver and all.

90 MALVOLIO: *[Reads]*

'Jove knows I love,
But who?
Lips, do not move,
No man must know.'

95 'No man must know.' What follows? the numbers alter'd!
'No man must know:' if this should be thee, Malvolio?

SIR TOBY: Marry, hang thee, brock![28]

[28]*badger*

MALVOLIO: *[Reads]*

'I may command where I adore;
But silence, like a Lucrece knife,
100 With bloodless stroke my heart doth gore;[29]
M, O, A, I, doth sway my life.'

[29]*stab*

FABIAN: A fustian[30] riddle!

[30]*lofty-sounding but ridiculous*

SIR TOBY: Excellent wench, say I.

MALVOLIO: 'M, O, A, I, doth sway my life.' Nay, but first, let
105 me see, let me see, let me see.

FABIAN: What dish o' poison has she dressed[31] him!

[31]*prepared*

SIR TOBY: And with what wing the staniel checks at it![32]

[32]*How quickly the hawk is distracted by it.*

MALVOLIO: 'I may command where I adore.' Why, she may command me: I serve her; she is my lady. Why, this is
110 evident to any formal capacity;[33] there is no obstruction[34] in this: and the end,—what should that alphabetical position portend? If I could make that resemble something in me,—Softly![35] M, O, A, I,—

[33]*normal intelligence*

[34]*difficulty*

[35]*Carefully*

SIR TOBY: O, ay, make up that:[36] he is now at a cold scent.[37]

[36]*put that together; solve that riddle*

[37]*a difficult trail to follow*

FABIAN: Sowter will cry upon't for all this, though it be as
115 rank as a fox.†

MALVOLIO: M,—Malvolio; M,—why, that begins my name.

FABIAN: Did not I say he would work it out? the cur is excellent at faults.†

MALVOLIO: M,—but then there is no consonancy[38] in the sequel;
120 that suffers under probation:[39] A should follow, but O does.
FABIAN: And O shall end, I hope.
SIR TOBY: Ay, or I'll cudgel[40] him, and make him cry 'O!'
MALVOLIO: And then I comes behind.
FABIAN: Ay, an you had any eye behind you, you might see more
125 detraction[41] at your heels than fortunes before you.
MALVOLIO: 'M, O, A, I; this simulation[42] is not as the former: and yet, to crush this a little, it would bow to me,[43] for every one of these letters are in my name. Soft! here follows prose: *[Reads]*

'If this fall into thy hand, revolve.[44] In my stars I am above
130 thee; but be not afraid of greatness: some are born great, some achieve greatness, and some have greatness thrust upon 'em. Thy Fates open their hands; let thy blood and spirit embrace them; and, to inure thyself to what thou art like to be,[45] cast thy humble slough[46] and appear fresh. Be opposite[47] with a
135 kinsman, surly with servants; let thy tongue tang[48] arguments of state;[49] put thyself into the trick of singularity:[50] she thus advises thee that sighs for thee. Remember who commended thy yellow stockings, and wished to see thee ever cross-gartered:† I say, remember. Go to, thou art made, if thou desirest
140 to be so; if not, let me see thee a steward still, the fellow of servants, and not worthy to touch Fortune's fingers. Farewell. She that would alter services[51] with thee,

The Fortunate-Unhappy.'

Daylight and champaign[52] discovers not more: this is open. I
145 will be proud, I will read politic authors, I will baffle[53] Sir Toby, I will wash off gross acquaintance, I will be point-devise[54] the very man. I do not now fool myself to let imagination jade[55] me; for every reason excites to this, that my lady loves me. She did commend my yellow stockings of late, she did praise my
150 leg being cross-gartered; and in this she manifests herself to my love, and with a kind of injunction drives me to these habits of her liking. I thank my stars I am happy. I will be strange,[56] stout,[57] in yellow stockings, and cross-gartered, even with the swiftness of putting on. Jove and my stars be praised! Here is yet a postscript:

155 *[Reads]* 'Thou canst not choose but know who I am. If thou entertainest my love, let it appear in thy smiling; thy smiles

[38]*agreement*
[39]*it gets weaker under examination*
[40]*beat with a club*
[41]*defamation, humiliation*
[42]*puzzle*
[43]*to force it a little, the letters would refer to me*
[44]*consider*
[45]*accustom yourself to what you will likely become*
[46]*skin*
[47]*argumentative*
[48]*echo with*
[49]*political theories*
[50]*eccentricity*
[51]*exchange positions*
[52]*open country*
[53]*punish, humiliate*
[54]*exactly, perfectly*
[55]*to make ridiculous*
[56]*aloof, distant*
[57]*brave*

become thee well; therefore, in my presence still smile, dear my sweet, I prithee.'

Jove, I thank thee. I will smile; I will do everything that
160 thou wilt have me. *[Exit.]*

FABIAN: I will not give my part of this sport for a pension of thousands to be paid from the Sophy.†

SIR TOBY: I could marry this wench for this device.[58]

[58] *scheme, plot*

SIR ANDREW: So could I too.

165 SIR TOBY: And ask no other dowry with her but such another jest.

SIR ANDREW: Nor I neither.

FABIAN: Here comes my noble gull-catcher.[59]

[59] *fool-catcher, trickster*

[Enter Maria.]

SIR TOBY: Wilt thou set thy foot o' my neck?†

170 SIR ANDREW: Or o' mine either?

SIR TOBY: Shall I play my freedom at traytrip,[60] and become thy bond-slave?

[60] *gamble my freedom at a game of dice*

SIR ANDREW: I' faith, or I either?

SIR TOBY: Why, thou hast put him in such a dream, that when
175 the image of it leaves him he must run mad.

MARIA: Nay, but say true; does it work upon him?

SIR TOBY: Like aqua-vitae with a midwife.†

MARIA: If you will then see the fruits of the sport, mark his first approach before my lady: he will come to her in
180 yellow stockings, and 'tis a colour she abhors, and cross-gartered, a fashion she detests; and he will smile upon her, which will now be so unsuitable to her disposition, being addicted to a melancholy as she is, that it cannot but turn him into a notable contempt;[61] if you will see it,
185 follow me.

[61] *state of being hated and scorned*

SIR TOBY: To the gates of Tartar,† thou most excellent devil of wit!

SIR ANDREW: I'll make one too.[62]

[62] *I'll go too*

[Exeunt.]

TWELFTH NIGHT
OR, WHAT YOU WILL

ACT III

SCENE I
Olivia's garden.

[Enter Viola, and Clown with a tabor.[1]]

VIOLA: Save thee,[2] friend, and thy music: dost thou live by[3] thy tabour?

CLOWN: No, sir, I live by the church.

VIOLA: Art thou a churchman?

5 CLOWN: No such matter, sir: I do live by the church; for I do live at my house, and my house doth stand by the church.

VIOLA: So thou mayst say, the king lies by a beggar, if a beggar dwell near him; or the church stands by thy tabour, if thy tabor stand by the church.†

10 CLOWN: You have said, sir. To see this age![4] A sentence is but a cheveril[5] glove to a good wit: how quickly the wrong side may be turned outward![6]

VIOLA: Nay, that's certain; they that dally nicely[7] with words may quickly make them wanton.[8]

15 CLOWN: I would, therefore,[9] my sister had had no name, sir.

VIOLA: Why, man?

CLOWN: Why, sir, her name's a word; and to dally with that word might make my sister wanton. But indeed words are very rascals, since bonds disgraced them.†

20 VIOLA: Thy reason, man?

CLOWN: Troth, sir, I can yield you none without words; and words are grown so false, I am loath[10] to prove reason with them.

VIOLA: I warrant[11] thou art a merry fellow and carest for

25 nothing.[12]

CLOWN: Not so, sir, I do care for something; but in my conscience, sir, I do not care for you: if that be to care for nothing, sir, I would it would make you invisible.

VIOLA: Art not thou the Lady Olivia's fool?

[1]*small drum*

[2]*God save you*

[3]*make a living by*

[4]*this time period*

[5]*a soft type of leather*

[6]*how quickly words can be turned inside out*

[7]*play artfully*

[8]*lewd*

[9]*I wish, then*

[10]*unwilling*

[11]*I attest; I pledge*

[12]*have no worries*

30 CLOWN: No, indeed, sir; the Lady Olivia has no folly: she will keep no fool, sir, till she be married; and fools are as like husbands as pilchards[13] are to herrings, the husband's the bigger: I am indeed not her fool, but her corrupter of words.

35 VIOLA: I saw thee late[14] at the Count Orsino's.

CLOWN: Foolery, sir, does walk about the orb[15] like the sun; it shines everywhere. I would be sorry, sir, but the fool should be as oft with your master as with my mistress: I think I saw your wisdom[16] there.

40 VIOLA: Nay, an thou pass upon me,[17] I'll no more with thee.[18] Hold,[19] there's expenses for thee.

CLOWN: Now Jove, in his next commodity[20] of hair, send thee a beard!

VIOLA: By my troth, I'll tell thee, I am almost sick for one;
45 *[Aside]* though I would not have it grow on my chin. *[to Clown]* Is thy lady within?

CLOWN: Would not a pair of these have bred,[21] sir?

VIOLA: Yes, being kept together and put to use.

CLOWN: I would play Lord Pandarus of Phrygia, sir, to bring
50 a Cressida to this Troilus.†

VIOLA: I understand you, sir; 'tis well begged.

CLOWN: The matter, I hope, is not great, sir, begging but a beggar: Cressida was a beggar.† My lady is within, sir. I will construe to them whence you come; who you are
55 and what you would are out of my welkin, I might say 'element,' but the word is over-worn. *[Exit.]*

VIOLA: This fellow's wise enough to play the fool;
And to do that well craves a kind of wit:
He must observe their mood on whom he jests,
60 The quality of persons, and the time,
And, like the haggard, check at every feather†
That comes before his eye. This is a practise
As full of labour as a wise man's art
For folly that he wisely shows, is fit;
65 But wise men, folly-fall'n,[22] quite taint their wit.†

[Enter Sir Toby and Sir Andrew.]

SIR TOBY: Save you,[23] gentleman.

VIOLA: And you, sir.

SIR ANDREW: *Dieu vous garde, monsieur.*[24]

[13] *small, herring-like fish*

[14] *recently*

[15] *the earth*

[16] *yourself, wise one*

[17] *if you drive at me with your jokes*

[18] *I'll speak no more with you.*

[19] *Take this*

[20] *shipment*

[21] *Might two of these coins have reproduced?*

[22] *who have fallen into folly*

[23] *God save you*

[24] *[French] May God protect you, sir.*

VIOLA: *Et vous aussi; votre serviteur.*[25]
70 SIR ANDREW: I hope, sir, you are; and I am yours.
SIR TOBY: Will you encounter[26] the house? my niece is desirous you should enter, if your trade[27] be to her.
VIOLA: I am bound to[28] your niece, sir; I mean, she is the list[29] of my voyage.
75 SIR TOBY: Taste[30] your legs, sir; put them to motion.
VIOLA: My legs do better understand me, sir, than I understand what you mean by bidding me taste my legs.
SIR TOBY: I mean, to go, sir, to enter.
VIOLA: I will answer you with gait and entrance. But we are
80 prevented.

[Enter Olivia and Maria.]

Most excellent accomplished lady, the heavens rain odours on you!
SIR ANDREW: That youth's a rare courtier: 'Rain odours'—well.
VIOLA: My matter hath no voice,[31] lady, but to your own most
85 pregnant[32] and vouchsafed ear.
SIR ANDREW: 'Odours,' 'pregnant,' and 'vouchsafed'—I'll get 'em all three ready.†
OLIVIA: Let the garden door be shut, and leave me to my hearing. *[Exeunt Sir Toby, Sir Andrew, and Maria.]*
90 Give me your hand, sir.
VIOLA: My duty, madam, and most humble service.
OLIVIA: What is your name?
VIOLA: Cesario is your servant's name, fair princess.
OLIVIA: My servant, sir? 'Twas never merry world,
95 Since lowly feigning was call'd compliment:†
You're servant to the Count Orsino, youth.
VIOLA: And he is yours, and his must needs be yours:[33]
Your servant's servant is your servant, madam.
OLIVIA: For him, I think not on him: for his thoughts,
100 Would they were blanks rather than fill'd with me!
VIOLA: Madam, I come to whet your gentle thoughts
On his behalf.
OLIVIA: O, by your leave, I pray you:
I bade you never speak again of him:
105 But, would you undertake another suit,[34]
I had rather hear you to solicit that
Than music from the spheres.†
VIOLA: Dear lady,—

[25] *[French] And you too, sir; I am your servant.*
[26] *go into*
[27] *business*
[28] *bound for*
[29] *goal*
[30] *Try*
[31] *cannot be told to anyone*
[32] *expert, clever*
[33] *his servant must necessarily be yours*
[34] *courtship*

OLIVIA: Give me leave, beseech you. I did send,
110 After the last enchantment you did here,[35]
A ring in chase of you:[36] so did I abuse
Myself, my servant and, I fear me, you:
Under your hard construction[37] must I sit,
To force that on you, in a shameful cunning,
115 Which you knew none of yours:[38] what might you think?
Have you not set mine honour at the stake,
And baited it with all the unmuzzled[39] thoughts
That tyrannous heart can think? To one of your
120 receiving[40]
Enough is shown: a cypress, not a bosom,
Hides my heart:† so let me hear you speak.

VIOLA: I pity you.

OLIVIA: That's a degree to love.

125 VIOLA: No, not a grize;[41] for 'tis a vulgar proof,[42]
That very oft we pity enemies.

OLIVIA: Why, then, methinks 'tis time to smile again.†
O, world, how apt the poor are to be proud!
If one should be a prey, how much the better
130 To fall before the lion than the wolf!† *[Clock strikes.]*
The clock upbraids[43] me with the waste of time.
Be not afraid, good youth, I will not have you:
And yet, when wit and youth is come to harvest,[44]
Your wife is like to reap[45] a proper man:
135 There lies your way, due west.

VIOLA: Then westward-ho!
Grace and good disposition attend your ladyship.
You'll nothing, madam, to my lord by me?[46]

OLIVIA: Stay. I prithee tell me what thou thinkest of me.

140 VIOLA: That you do think you are not what you are.†

OLIVIA: If I think so, I think the same of you.

VIOLA: Then think you right: I am not what I am.

OLIVIA: I would you were as I would have you be!

VIOLA: Would it be better, madam, than I am?
145 I wish it might, for now I am your fool.

OLIVIA: *[Aside.]* O what a deal[47] of scorn looks beautiful
In the contempt and anger of his lip!
A murderous guilt shows not itself more soon
Than love that would seem hid: love's night is noon.†
150 Cesario, by the roses of the spring,

[35] *After the last time you charmed me*

[36] *after you*

[37] *interpretation*

[38] *Which you knew was not yours (meaning the ring)*

[39] *unrestrained*

[40] *capacity to understand; intelligence*

[41] *a degree*

[42] *a common experience*

[43] *reproaches, reprimands*

[44] *has grown up*

[45] *likely to obtain*

[46] *You have no message for my lord?*

[47] *great deal*

By maidhood, honour, truth, and everything,
I love thee so, that, maugre[48] all thy pride,
Nor wit nor reason can my passion hide.
Do not extort thy reasons from this clause,
For that I woo thou therefore hast no cause,
155 But rather reason thus with reason fetter,
Love sought is good, but given unsought is better.†

VIOLA: By innocence I swear, and by my youth
I have one heart, one bosom, and one truth,
And that no woman has; nor never none
160 Shall mistress be of it, save I alone.
And so adieu, good madam: never more
Will I my master's tears to you deplore.[49]

OLIVIA: Yet come again; for thou perhaps, mayst move
That heart, which now abhors, to like his love.

[Exeunt.]

[48] *despite*

[49] *complain about*

SCENE II
Olivia's house.

[Enter Sir Toby, Sir Andrew, and Fabian.]

SIR ANDREW: No, faith, I'll not stay a jot longer.

SIR TOBY: Thy reason, dear venom;[1] give thy reason.

FABIAN: You must needs yield your reason, Sir Andrew.

SIR ANDREW: Marry, I saw your niece do more favours to the
5 Count's serving-man than ever she bestowed upon me; I saw't i' the orchard.

SIR TOBY: Did she see thee the while, old boy? tell me that.

SIR ANDREW: As plain as I see you now.

FABIAN: This was a great argument of love in her toward you.

10 SIR ANDREW: 'Slight,[2] will you make an ass o' me?

FABIAN: I will prove it legitimate, sir, upon the oaths of judgment and reason.

SIR TOBY: And they have been grand-jurymen since before Noah was a sailor.

15 FABIAN: She did show favour to the youth in your sight only to exasperate you, to awake your dormouse valour,[3] to put fire in your heart and brimstone in your liver. You should then have accosted her; and with some excellent jests, fire-new

[1] *venomous one*

[2] *By God's light*

[3] *quiet bravery*

[4]beaten
[5]neglected
[6]strategy
[7]would just as much like to

from the mint, you should have banged[4] the youth into
20 dumbness. This was looked for at your hand, and this
was balked:[5] the double gilt of this opportunity you let
time wash off, and you are now sailed into the north of
my lady's opinion; where you will hang like an icicle on
a Dutchman's beard,† unless you do redeem it by some
25 laudable attempt either of valour or policy.[6]

SIR ANDREW: And't be any way, it must be with valour; for
policy I hate: I had as lief[7] be a Brownist as a politician.†

SIR TOBY: Why, then, build me thy fortunes upon the basis of
valour. Challenge me the Count's youth to fight with him;
30 hurt him in eleven places; my niece shall take note of it;
and assure thyself, there is no love-broker in the world
can more prevail in man's commendation with woman
than report of valour.

FABIAN: There is no way but this, Sir Andrew.

35 SIR ANDREW: Will either of you bear me a challenge to him?

[8]harsh
[9]creativity
[10]freedom
[11]go about it
[12]bedchamber

SIR TOBY: Go, write it in a martial hand; be curst[8] and brief;
it is no matter how witty, so it be eloquent and full of
invention:[9] taunt him with the licence[10] of ink: if thou
'thou'st' him some thrice, it shall not be amiss;† and as
40 many lies as will lie in thy sheet of paper, although the
sheet were big enough for the bed of Ware in England,†
set 'em down: go about it. Let there be gall enough in
thy ink, though thou write with a goose-pen,† no matter.
About it.[11]

45 SIR ANDREW: Where shall I find you?

SIR TOBY: We'll call thee at the cubiculo.[12] Go.

[Exit Sir Andrew.]

[13]little man
[14]I have cost him a lot of money

FABIAN: This is a dear manakin[13] to you, Sir Toby.

SIR TOBY: I have been dear to him,[14] lad, some two thousand
strong, or so.

50 FABIAN: We shall have a rare letter from him: but you'll not
deliver't.

[15]wagon ropes
[16]haul
[17]prediction

SIR TOBY: Never trust me, then; and by all means stir on the
youth to an answer. I think oxen and wainropes[15] cannot
hale[16] them together. For Andrew, if he were opened, and
55 you find so much blood in his liver as will clog the foot
of a flea, I'll eat the rest of the anatomy.†

FABIAN: And his opposite, the youth, bears in his visage no
great presage[17] of cruelty.

[Enter Maria.]

SIR TOBY: Look, where the youngest wren of nine† comes.

60 MARIA: If you desire the spleen,† and will laugh yourselves into stitches, follow me. Yond gull[18] Malvolio is turned heathen, a very renegado;[19] for there is no Christian, that means to be saved by believing rightly, can ever believe such impossible passages of grossness.[20] He's in yellow stockings.

65 SIR TOBY: And cross-gartered?

MARIA: Most villainously;[21] like a pedant[22] that keeps a school i' the church. I have dogged him, like his murderer. He does obey every point of the letter that I dropped to betray him: he does smile his face into more lines than is in the new 70 map with the augmentation of the Indies:† you have not seen such a thing as 'tis; I can hardly forbear[23] hurling things at him. I know my lady will strike him: if she do, he'll smile and take't for a great favour.

SIR TOBY: Come, bring us, bring us where he is.

[Exeunt.]

[18]*That fool*

[19]*renegade*

[20]*stupidity*

[21]*in an evil way*

[22]*schoolteacher*

[23]*restrain myself from*

SCENE III
A street.

[Enter Sebastian and Antonio.]

SEBASTIAN: I would not by my will have troubled you;
But, since you make your pleasure of your pains,
I will no further chide you.

ANTONIO: I could not stay behind you: my desire,
5 More sharp than filed steel, did spur me forth;
And not all love to see you, though so much
As might have drawn one to a longer voyage,
But jealousy[1] what might befall your travel,
Being skilless in these parts; which to a stranger,
10 Unguided and unfriended, often prove
Rough and unhospitable: my willing love,
The rather by these arguments of fear,
Set forth in your pursuit.[2]

SEBASTIAN: My kind Antonio,
15 I can no other answer make but thanks,
And thanks; and ever oft good turns

[1]*suspicion, apprehension*

[2]*My fear for your safety is what made me pursue you.*

Are shuffled off with such uncurrent pay:
But, were my worth as is my conscience firm,
You should find better dealing.† What's to do?
20 Shall we go see the reliques[3] of this town?

ANTONIO: Tomorrow, sir; best, first, go see your lodging.[4]

SEBASTIAN: I am not weary, and 'tis long to night:
I pray you, let us satisfy our eyes
With the memorials and the things of fame
25 That do renown this city.[5]

ANTONIO: Would you'd pardon me;
I do not without danger walk these streets:
Once, in a sea-fight, 'gainst the Count his galleys[6]
I did some service;[7] of such note indeed,
30 That were I ta'en here it would scarce be answer'd.[8]

SEBASTIAN: Belike you slew[9] great number of his people.

ANTONIO: The offence is not of such a bloody nature;
Albeit[10] the quality of the time and quarrel
Might well have given us bloody argument.
35 It might have since been answer'd in repaying
What we took from them; which, for traffic's sake,[11]
Most of our city did: only myself stood out;
For which, if I be lapsed[12] in this place,
I shall pay dear.

40 SEBASTIAN: Do not then walk too open.[13]

ANTONIO: It doth not fit me. Hold,[14] sir, here's my purse.
In the south suburbs, at the Elephant,†
Is best to lodge: I will bespeak our diet,[15]
Whiles you beguile the time and feed your knowledge
45 With viewing of the town: there shall you have me.[16]

SEBASTIAN: Why I your purse?[17]

ANTONIO: Haply[18] your eye shall light upon some toy
You have desire to purchase; and your store,[19]
I think, is not for idle markets,[20] sir.

50 SEBASTIAN: I'll be your purse-bearer, and leave you
For an hour.

ANTONIO: To the Elephant.

SEBASTIAN: I do remember.

[Exeunt.]

[3]*remnants, scraps*

[4]*first, find a place to stay*

[5]*that make this city well-known*

[6]*against the count's boats*

[7]*military fighting*

[8]*it would be hard to explain*

[9]*It sounds like you killed*

[10]*Although*

[11]*for the sake of trade or commerce*

[12]*caught by surprise*

[13]*openly, conspicuously*

[14]*Take this*

[15]*order our meals*

[16]*you will find me*

[17]*Why do you give me your purse?*

[18]*Perhaps*

[19]*the money you have*

[20]*useless purchases*

SCENE IV
Olivia's garden.

[Enter Olivia and Maria.]

OLIVIA: *[Aside]* I have sent after him: he says he'll come;
How shall I feast[1] him? what bestow on him?[2]
For youth is bought more oft than begg'd or borrow'd.†
I speak too loud.
5 *[To Maria.]* Where's Malvolio? he is sad and civil,
And suits well for a servant with my fortunes:
Where is Malvolio?

MARIA: He's coming, madam; but in very strange manner. He is, sure possessed, madam.

10 OLIVIA: Why, what's the matter? does he rave?

MARIA: No, madam, he does nothing but smile: your ladyship were best to have some guard about you, if he come; for, sure, the man is tainted in his wits.[3]

OLIVIA: Go call him hither. *[Exit Maria.]* I'm as mad as he,
15 If sad and merry madness equal be.

[Enter Malvolio, with Maria.]

How now, Malvolio?

MALVOLIO: Sweet lady, ho, ho.

OLIVIA: Smil'st thou? I sent for thee upon a sad occasion.

MALVOLIO: Sad, lady? I could be sad: this does make some
20 obstruction in the blood,[4] this cross-gartering; but what of that? If it please the eye of one, it is with me as the very true sonnet is, 'Please one and please all.'†

OLIVIA: Why, how dost thou, man? what is the matter with thee?

25 MALVOLIO: Not black[5] in my mind, though yellow in my legs. It did come to his hands, and commands shall be executed: I think we do know the sweet Roman hand.†

OLIVIA: Wilt thou go to bed, Malvolio?

MALVOLIO: To bed? 'Ay, sweetheart, and I'll come to thee.'

30 OLIVIA: God comfort thee! Why dost thou smile so, and kiss thy hand so oft?

MARIA: How do you, Malvolio?

MALVOLIO: At your request? yes; nightingales answer daws.†

[1] *entertain*

[2] *What should I give him?*

[3] *flawed in his mental capacities*

[4] *circulation*

[5] *sad, mourning*

35 MARIA: Why appear you with this ridiculous boldness before my lady?

MALVOLIO: 'Be not afraid of greatness:' 'twas well writ.

OLIVIA: What meanest thou by that, Malvolio?

MALVOLIO: 'Some are born great,'—

40 OLIVIA: Ha?

MALVOLIO: 'Some achieve greatness,'—

OLIVIA: What say'st thou?

MALVOLIO: 'And some have greatness thrust upon them.'

OLIVIA: Heaven restore thee![6]

45 MALVOLIO: 'Remember who commended thy yellow stockings,'—

OLIVIA: 'Thy yellow stockings'?

MALVOLIO: 'And wished to see thee cross-gartered.'

OLIVIA: 'Cross-gartered'?

50 MALVOLIO: 'Go to, thou an made, if thou desirest to be so:'—

OLIVIA: Am I made?

MALVOLIO: 'If not, let me see thee a servant still.'

OLIVIA: Why, this is very midsummer madness.†

[Enter Servant.]

SERVANT: Madam, the young gentleman of the Count Orsino's
55 is returned: I could hardly entreat him back: he attends your ladyship's pleasure.

OLIVIA: I'll come to him. *[Exit Servant.]*
Good Maria, let this fellow be looked to.[7] Where's my cousin Toby? Let some of my people have a special care
60 of him: I would not have him miscarry[8] for the half of my dowry.[9] *[Exeunt Olivia and Maria.]*

MALVOLIO: O, ho! do you come near me now? No worse man than Sir Toby to look to me! This concurs directly with the letter: she sends him on purpose, that I may appear
65 stubborn to him; for she incites me to that in the letter. 'Cast thy humble slough,' says she; 'be opposite with a kinsman, surly with servants; let thy tongue tang with arguments of state; put thyself into the trick of singularity'; and consequently sets down the manner how; as, a
70 sad face, a reverend carriage,[10] a slow tongue, in the habit of some sir of note,[11] and so forth. I have limed her;† but it is Jove's doing, and Jove make me thankful! And, when she went away now, 'Let this fellow be looked to':

[6] *Heaven help you!*

[7] *looked after; cared for*

[8] *be harmed*

[9] *property*

[10] *a respectable manner*

[11] *in the clothing of a gentleman*

Fellow! not Malvolio, nor after my degree,[12] but fellow. Why,
75 everything adheres together, that no dram of a scruple, no scruple of a scruple, no obstacle, no incredulous or unsafe circumstance—What can be said? Nothing that can be, can come between me and the full prospect of my hopes. Well, Jove, not I, is the doer of this, and he is to be thanked.

[12]*position*

[Re-enter Maria, with Sir Toby and Fabian.]

80 **SIR TOBY:** Which way is he, in the name of sanctity?[13] If all the devils of hell be drawn in little, and Legion† himself possessed him, yet I'll speak to him.

[13]*holiness*

FABIAN: Here he is, here he is. How is't with you, sir? how is't with you, man?

85 **MALVOLIO:** Go off; I discard you: let me enjoy my private.[14] Go off.

[14]*privacy*

MARIA: Lo, how hollow[15] the fiend speaks within him! did not I tell you? Sir Toby, my lady prays you to have a care of him.

[15]*deep and low*

MALVOLIO: Ah, ha! does she so?

90 **SIR TOBY:** Go to, go to; peace, peace; we must deal gently with him: let me alone. How do you, Malvolio? how is't with you? What, man! defy the devil: consider, he's an enemy to mankind.

MALVOLIO: Do you know what you say?

95 **MARIA:** La you,[16] an you speak ill of the devil, how he takes it at heart! Pray God, he be not bewitched!

[16]*Look you!*

FABIAN: Carry his water to the wise woman.†

MARIA: Marry, and it shall be done tomorrow morning, if I live. My lady would not lose him[17] for more than I'll say.

[17]*would not want to lose him*

100 **MALVOLIO:** How now, mistress!

MARIA: O Lord!

SIR TOBY: Prithee, hold thy peace; this is not the way: do you not see you move[18] him? let me alone with him.

[18]*agitate*

FABIAN: No way but gentleness; gently, gently: the fiend is rough,
105 and will not be roughly used.[19]

[19]*treated*

SIR TOBY: Why, how now, my bawcock?[20] how dost thou, chuck.[21]

[20]*good fellow*

[21]*chick (an endearing term)*

MALVOLIO: Sir!

SIR TOBY: Ay, Biddy,[22] come with me. What, man! 'tis not for
110 gravity to play at cherry-pit with Satan: hang him, foul collier!†

[22]*Chicken*

MARIA: Get him to say his prayers, good Sir Toby, get him to pray.

MALVOLIO: My prayers, minx![23]

[23]*reckless woman*

115 MARIA: No, I warrant you, he will not hear of godliness.

MALVOLIO: Go, hang yourselves all! you are idle shallow things: I am not of your element.[24] You shall know more hereafter. *[Exit.]*

[24]*I am not like you*

SIR TOBY: Is't possible?

120 FABIAN: If this were played upon a stage now, I could condemn it as an improbable fiction.

SIR TOBY: His very genius[25] hath taken the infection of the device,[26] man.

[25]*spirit*

[26]*scheme*

MARIA: Nay, pursue him now; lest the device take air and
125 taint.[27]

[27]*become exposed and get ruined*

FABIAN: Why, we shall make him mad indeed.

MARIA: The house will be the quieter.

SIR TOBY: Come, we'll have him in a dark room and bound.† My niece is already in the belief that he's mad; we may
130 carry it thus,[28] for our pleasure and his penance, till our very pastime,[29] tired out of breath, prompt us to have mercy on him: at which time we will bring the device to the bar,[30] and crown thee for a finder of madmen. But see, but see.

[28]*keep it going like this*

[29]*amusement*

[30]*the courtroom*

[Enter Sir Andrew.]

135 FABIAN: More matter for a May morning.

SIR ANDREW: Here's the challenge, read it. I warrant there's vinegar and pepper in't.[31]

FABIAN: Is't so saucy?[32]

SIR ANDREW: Ay, is't, I warrant[33] him: do but read.

[31]*It's filled with bold words.*

[32]*pungent*

[33]*assure*

140 SIR TOBY: Give me. *[Reads]* 'Youth, whatsoever thou art, thou art but a scurvy fellow.'

FABIAN: Good and valiant.

SIR TOBY: *[Reads]* 'Wonder not, nor admire not in thy mind, why I do call thee so, for I will show thee no reason for't.'

145 FABIAN: A good note; that keeps you from the blow of the law.[34]

[34]*being held legally responsible*

SIR TOBY: *[Reads]* 'Thou comest to the Lady Olivia, and in my sight she uses thee kindly: but thou liest in thy throat; that is not the matter I challenge thee for.'

150 FABIAN: Very brief, and to exceeding good sense *[aside]* —less.

SIR TOBY: *[Reads]* 'I will waylay thee going home; where if it be thy chance to kill me,'—

FABIAN: Good.

SIR TOBY: *[Reads]* 'Thou killest me like a rogue and a villain.'

155 FABIAN: Still you keep o' the windy[35] side of the law. Good.

SIR TOBY: *[Reads]* 'Fare thee well; and God have mercy upon one of our souls! He may have mercy upon mine; but my hope is better, and so look to thyself. Thy friend, as thou usest him, and thy sworn enemy,

160 Andrew Aguecheek.'

If this letter move him not, his legs cannot: I'll give't him.

MARIA: You may have very fit occasion for't; he is now in some commerce[36] with my lady, and will by and by depart.

SIR TOBY: Go, Sir Andrew; scout me for him[37] at the corner of the

165 orchard, like a bum-baily:[38] so soon as ever thou seest him, draw;[39] and, as thou drawest, swear horrible; for it comes to pass oft that a terrible oath, with a swaggering accent sharply twanged off,[40] gives manhood more approbation[41] than ever proof itself would have earned him. Away!

170 SIR ANDREW: Nay, let me alone for swearing. *[Exit.]*

SIR TOBY: Now will not I deliver his letter: for the behaviour of the young gentleman gives him out to be of good capacity and breeding; his employment between his lord and my niece confirms no less; therefore, this letter, being so excel-

175 lently ignorant, will breed no terror in the youth: he will find it comes from a clodpole.[42] But, sir, I will deliver his challenge by word of mouth; set upon Aguecheek notable report of valour, and drive the gentleman, as I know his youth will aptly receive it, into a most hideous opinion of his rage, skill,

180 fury, and impetuosity. This will so fright them both that they will kill one another by the look, like cockatrices.†

[Enter Olivia and Viola.]

FABIAN: Here he comes with your niece: give them way[43] till he take leave, and presently after him.

SIR TOBY: I will meditate the while upon some horrid message for

185 a challenge. *[Exeunt Sir Toby, Fabian, and Maria.]*

OLIVIA: I have said too much unto a heart of stone
And laid mine honour too unchary on't:[44]

[35] *safe*

[36] *business*

[37] *watch for him*

[38] *an arresting officer*

[39] *draw your sword*

[40] *sharply spoken*

[41] *confirmation; ratification*

[42] *blockhead, fool*

[43] *leave them alone*

[44] *carelessly*

There's something in me that reproves my fault;[45]
But such a headstrong potent fault it is,
190 That it but mocks reproof.

VIOLA: With the same 'havior that your passion bears
Goes on my master's grief.[46]

OLIVIA: Here, wear this jewel for me, 'tis my picture;
Refuse it not; it hath no tongue to vex you;
195 And, I beseech you, come again tomorrow.
What shall you ask of me that I'll deny,
That honour, saved, may upon asking give?†

VIOLA: Nothing but this; your true love for my master.

OLIVIA: How with mine honour may I give him that
200 Which I have given to you?

VIOLA: I will acquit[47] you.

OLIVIA: Well, come again tomorrow. Fare thee well;
A fiend like thee might bear my soul to hell. *[Exit.]*

[Re-enter Sir Toby and Fabian.]

SIR TOBY: Gentleman, God save thee.

205 VIOLA: And you, sir.

SIR TOBY: That defence thou hast, betake thee to't.[48] Of what nature the wrongs are thou hast done him, I know not; but thy intercepter, full of despite,[49] bloody as the hunter, attends thee at the orchard end: dismount thy tuck,[50] be
210 yare[51] in thy preparation, for thy assailant is quick, skilful, and deadly.

VIOLA: You mistake, sir; I am sure no man hath any quarrel to me: my remembrance is very free and clear from any image of offence done to any man.

215 SIR TOBY: You'll find it otherwise, I assure you: therefore, if you hold your life at any price, betake you to your guard; for your opposite hath in him what youth, strength, skill, and wrath can furnish man withal.

VIOLA: I pray you, sir, what is he?

220 SIR TOBY: He is knight, dubbed with unhatched rapier and on carpet consideration;† but he is a devil in private brawl: souls and bodies hath he divorced three;[52] and his incensement[53] at this moment is so implacable, that satisfaction can be none but by pangs of death and sepulchre.
225 Hob, nob[54] is his word; give't or take't.

VIOLA: I will return again into the house and desire some conduct[55] of the lady. I am no fighter. I have heard of some

[45] *reprimands me for my mistake*

[46] *my master's grief continues*

[47] *set you free from obligation*

[48] *prepare yourself for it*

[49] *scorn*

[50] *draw your sword*

[51] *quick*

[52] *he has killed three men*

[53] *anger*

[54] *have or have not; hit or miss*

[55] *escort, guard*

kind of men that put quarrels purposely on others to taste their valour: belike[56] this is a man of that quirk.

230 SIR TOBY: Sir, no; his indignation derives itself[57] out of a very competent[58] injury; therefore, get you on and give him his desire. Back you shall not to the house, unless you undertake that with me which with as much safety you might answer him:[59] therefore, on, or strip your sword stark

235 naked; for meddle[60] you must, that's certain, or forswear to wear iron about you.†

VIOLA: This is as uncivil as strange. I beseech you, do me this courteous office,[61] as to know of the knight what my offence to him is: it is something of my negligence, nothing of my

240 purpose.

SIR TOBY: I will do so. Signior Fabian, stay you by this gentleman till my return. *[Exit.]*

VIOLA: Pray you, sir, do you know of this matter?

FABIAN: I know the knight is incensed against you, even to

245 a mortal arbitrement;[62] but nothing of the circumstance more.

VIOLA: I beseech you, what manner of man is he?

FABIAN: Nothing of that wonderful promise, to read him by his form, as you are like to find him in the proof of his

250 valour.[63] He is indeed, sir, the most skilful, bloody, and fatal opposite[64] that you could possibly have found in any part of Illyria. Will you walk towards him? I will make your peace with him if I can.

VIOLA: I shall be much bound[65] to you for't. I am one that would

255 rather go with sir priest than sir knight:[66] I care not who knows so much of my mettle. *[Exeunt.]*

[Re-enter Sir Toby With Sir Andrew.]

SIR TOBY: Why, man, he's a very devil; I have not seen such a virago.† I had a pass[67] with him, rapier, scabbard, and all, and he gives me the stuck-in[68] with such a mortal motion,

260 that it is inevitable; and on the answer, he pays you[69] as surely as your feet hit the ground they step on. They say he has been fencer to the Sophy.[70]

SIR ANDREW: Pox on't,† I'll not meddle with him.

SIR TOBY: Ay, but he will not now be pacified: Fabian can scarce

265 hold him yonder.

SIR ANDREW: Plague on't, an I thought he had been valiant, and

[56] *it seems like*

[57] *originates*

[58] *sufficient*

[59] *unless you want to fight with me, which would be just as bad for you*

[60] *take on; engage*

[61] *kind service; favor*

[62] *deadly decision or judgment*

[63] *Nothing great in physical appearance, but extremely brave.*

[64] *adversary*

[65] *obliged, grateful*

[66] *I am more of the religious kind than the fighting kind.*

[67] *bout of sword-fighting*

[68] *thrust*

[69] *on the return hit, he strikes you*

[70] *the King of Persia*

so cunning in fence, I'd have seen him damned ere I'd have challenged him. Let him let the matter slip, and I'll give him my horse, grey Capilet.

270 SIR TOBY: I'll make the motion:[71] stand here, make a good show on't: this shall end without the perdition of souls. *[Aside.]* Marry, I'll ride your horse as well as I ride you.

[Re-enter Fabian and Viola.]

[Aside to Fabian] I have his horse to take up[72] the quarrel: I have persuaded him the youth's a devil.

275 FABIAN: He is as horribly conceited of him;[73] and pants and looks pale, as if a bear were at his heels.

SIR TOBY: *[To Viola]* There's no remedy, sir; he will fight with you for's oath[74] sake: marry, he hath better bethought him of his quarrel,[75] and he finds that now scarce[76] to be

280 worth talking of: therefore draw, for the supportance of his vow; he protests[77] he will not hurt you.

VIOLA: *[Aside]* Pray God defend me! A little thing would make me tell them how much I lack of a man.

FABIAN: Give ground, if you see him furious.

285 SIR TOBY: Come, Sir Andrew, there's no remedy; the gentleman will, for his honour's sake, have one bout with you; he cannot by the duello[78] avoid it; but he has promised me, as he is a gentleman and a soldier, he will not hurt you. Come on: to't.

290 SIR ANDREW: Pray God, he keep his oath! *[Draws]*

VIOLA: I do assure you 'tis against my will. *[Draws]*

[Enter Antonio.]

ANTONIO: Put up your sword. If this young gentleman
Have done offence, I take the fault on me:[79]
If you offend him, I for him defy you.[80]

295 SIR TOBY: You, sir! why, what are you?

ANTONIO: One, sir, that for his love dares yet do more
Than you have heard him brag to you he will.

SIR TOBY: Nay, if you be an undertaker,[81] I am for you.[82] *[Draws]*

[Enter two Officers.]

FABIAN: O good Sir Toby, hold! here come the officers.

[71] *proposal, request*

[72] *to settle*

[73] *Cesario is just as fearful of him*

[74] *for the sake of his word or promise*

[75] *he has thought better of whatever he was angry about*

[76] *barely*

[77] *promises*

[78] *standard rules of dueling*

[79] *I'll take responsibility for it*

[80] *I challenge you for his sake.*

[81] *a taker of challenges*

[82] *I'll fight with you.*

300 SIR TOBY: *[To Antonio.]* I'll be with you anon.

VIOLA: *[To Sir Andrew.]* Pray, sir, put your sword up, if you please.

SIR ANDREW: Marry, will I, sir; and, for that[83] I promised you, I'll be as good as my word: he will bear you easily and reins
305 well.[84]

FIRST OFFICER: This is the man; do thy office.

SECOND OFFICER: Antonio, I arrest thee at the suit of Count Orsino.

ANTONIO: You do mistake me, sir.

310 FIRST OFFICER: No, sir, no jot.[85] I know your favour[86] well,
Though now you have no sea-cap on your head.
Take him away: he knows I know him well.

ANTONIO: I must obey. *[To Viola.]* This comes with seeking you:
315 But there's no remedy; I shall answer it.
What will you do, now my necessity
Makes me to ask you for my purse? It grieves me
Much more for what I cannot do for you
Than what befalls myself. You stand amazed;
320 But be of comfort.[87]

SECOND OFFICER: Come, sir, away.

ANTONIO: *[To Viola.]* I must entreat of you some of that money.

VIOLA: What money, sir?
For the fair kindness you have show'd me here,
325 And, part, being prompted by your present trouble,
Out of my lean and low ability[88]
I'll lend you something: my having[89] is not much;
I'll make division of my present[90] with you:
Hold, there is half my coffer.

330 ANTONIO: Will you deny me now?
Is't possible that my deserts to you[91]
Can lack persuasion? Do not tempt my misery,
Lest that it make me so unsound[92] a man
As to upbraid[93] you with those kindnesses
335 That I have done for you.

VIOLA: I know of none,
Nor know I you by voice or any feature:
I hate ingratitude more in a man
Than lying, vainness, babbling, drunkenness,
340 Or any taint of vice[94] whose strong corruption
Inhabits our frail blood.

[83] *the horse*

[84] *He rides well and behaves.*

[85] *not a bit*

[86] *face*

[87] *be consoled; be cheerful*

[88] *meager wealth*

[89] *what I have*

[90] *what I have right now*

[91] *what I've done for you*

[92] *unprincipled*

[93] *criticize*

[94] *stain of sin*

Antonio: O heavens themselves!
Second Officer: Come, sir, I pray you go.
Antonio: Let me speak a little. This youth that you see here
345 I snatch'd one half out of the jaws of death,
Relieved him with such sanctity of love,
And to his image, which methought did promise
Most venerable worth, did I devotion.[95]
First Officer: What's that to us? The time goes by: away!
350 Antonio: But O how vile an idol proves this god!
Thou hast, Sebastian, done good feature[96] shame.
In nature there's no blemish but the mind;
None can be call'd deform'd but the unkind:
Virtue is beauty, but the beauteous evil
355 Are empty trunks, o'erflourished[97] by the devil.
First Officer: The man grows mad; away with him. Come, come, sir.
Antonio: Lead me on. *[Exeunt Officers with Antonio.]*
Viola: *[Aside]* Methinks his words do from such passion
360 fly[98]
That he believes himself: so do not I.[99]
Prove true, imagination, O, prove true,
That I, dear brother, be now ta'en for you!†
Sir Toby: Come hither, knight; come hither, Fabian: we'll
365 whisper o'er a couplet or two of most sage saws.[100]
Viola: He named Sebastian:[101] I my brother know
Yet living in my glass;[102] even such and so
In favour was my brother;[103] and he went
Still in this fashion,[104] colour, ornament,
370 For him I imitate: O, if it prove,
Tempests are kind and salt waves fresh in love! *[Exit.]*
Sir Toby: *[To Sir Andrew.]* A very dishonest paltry boy, and more a coward than a hare:† his dishonesty appears in leaving his friend here in necessity and denying him; and
375 for his cowardship, ask Fabian.
Fabian: A coward, a most devout coward, religious in it.
Sir Andrew: 'Slid,[105] I'll after him again and beat him.
Sir Toby: Do; cuff him soundly, but never draw thy sword.
Sir Andrew: And I do not,— *[Exit.]*
380 Fabian: Come, let's see the event.
Sir Toby: I dare lay any money 'twill be nothing yet.[106]

[Exeunt.]

[95] *I devoted myself to*

[96] *appearance*

[97] *varnished over; made to look nice*

[98] *proceed, ensue*

[99] *I don't believe him, but I would like to.*

[100] *wise sayings*

[101] *He called me Sebastian*

[102] *I see my brother when I look in the mirror*

[103] *his face was just like mine*

[104] *he always dressed like this*

[105] *By God's eyelid (an exclamation)*

[106] *I bet it will still amount to nothing.*

Twelfth Night
or, What You Will

ACT IV

SCENE I
Before Olivia's house.

[Enter Sebastian and Clown.]

CLOWN: Will you make me believe that I am not sent for you?[1]
SEBASTIAN: Go to, go to, thou art a foolish fellow;
Let me be clear of thee.[2]
CLOWN: Well held out,[3] i' faith! No, I do not know you; nor I am
5 not sent to you by my lady, to bid you come speak with her; nor your name is not Master Cesario; nor this is not my nose neither. Nothing that is so is so.
SEBASTIAN: I prithee, vent thy folly somewhere else: Thou know'st not me.
10 CLOWN: Vent my folly! he has heard that word of some great man and now applies it to a fool. Vent my folly! I am afraid this great lubber,[4] the world, will prove a cockney.[5] I prithee now, ungird thy strangeness[6] and tell me what I shall vent to my lady: shall I vent to her that thou art coming?
15 SEBASTIAN: I prithee, foolish Greek,[7] depart from me:
There's money for thee: if you tarry longer,
I shall give worse payment.
CLOWN: By my troth, thou hast an open hand.[8] These wise men that give fools money get themselves a good report—after
20 fourteen years' purchase.†

[Enter Sir Andrew, Sir Toby, and Fabian.]

SIR ANDREW: *[To Sebastian.]* Now, sir, have I met you again? *[Striking Sebastian.]* there's for you.
SEBASTIAN: Why, there's for thee, and there, and there. Are all the people mad? *[Beating Sir Andrew.]*
25 SIR TOBY: Hold, sir, or I'll throw your dagger o'er the house.

[1] *I haven't been ordered to get you?*

[2] *Leave me alone.*

[3] *Well kept up*

[4] *rude person*

[5] *clueless person*

[6] *let loose your aloofness*

[7] *merry fellow*

[8] *a generous nature*

CLOWN: This will I tell my lady straight. I would not be in some of your coats[9] for two pence. *[Exit Clown.]*

SIR TOBY: Come on, sir; hold. *[Holding Sebastian.]*

SIR ANDREW: Nay, let him alone: I'll go another way to work
30 with him; I'll have an action of battery[10] against him, if there be any law in Illyria: though I struck him first, yet it's no matter for that.[11]

SEBASTIAN: Let go thy hand.[12]

SIR TOBY: Come, sir, I will not let you go. Come, my young
35 soldier, put up your iron: you are well fleshed;† come on.

SEBASTIAN: I will be free from thee. What wouldst thou now?
If thou dar'st tempt me further, draw thy sword.

SIR TOBY: What, what? Nay, then I must have an ounce or two
40 of this malapert[13] blood from you. *[Draws.]*

[Enter Olivia.]

OLIVIA: Hold, Toby; on thy life, I charge thee hold.

SIR TOBY: Madam!

OLIVIA: Will it be ever thus? Ungracious wretch,
Fit for the mountains and the barbarous caves,
45 Where manners ne'er were preach'd! Out of my sight!
Be not offended, dear Cesario.
Rudesby,[14] be gone!
[Exeunt Sir Toby, Sir Andrew, and Fabian.]
I pr'ythee, gentle friend,
Let thy fair wisdom, not thy passion, sway[15]
50 In this uncivil and unjust extent[16]
Against thy peace. Go with me to my house,
And hear thou there how many fruitless[17] pranks
This ruffian hath botch'd up, that thou thereby
55 Mayst smile at this: thou shalt not choose but go;
Do not deny. Beshrew his soul for me,
He started one poor heart of mine in thee.†

SEBASTIAN: What relish[18] is in this? how runs the stream?[19]
Or I am mad, or else this is a dream:
60 Let fancy still my sense in Lethe† steep;
If it be thus to dream, still let me sleep!

OLIVIA: Nay, come, I prithee; would thou'dst be ruled by me!

SEBASTIAN: Madam, I will.

[9] I would not be in your shoes

[10] accuse him of assault

[11] it doesn't matter

[12] Take your hands off me.

[13] rude, impudent

[14] Brute

[15] rule

[16] display

[17] empty, idle; worthless

[18] pleasant taste

[19] where is this going?

OLIVIA: O, say so, and so be! *[Exeunt.]*

SCENE II
Olivia's house.

[Enter Maria and Clown.]

MARIA: Nay, I prithee, put on this gown and this beard; make him believe thou art Sir Topas the curate. Do it quickly; I'll call Sir Toby the whilst.[1] *[Exit Maria.]*

CLOWN: Well, I'll put it on, and I will dissemble[2] myself in't; and
5 I would I were the first that ever dissembled in such a gown. I am not tall enough to become the function[3] well, nor lean enough to be thought a good student; but to be said an honest man and a good housekeeper[4] goes as fairly as to say a careful man and a great scholar. The competitors[5] enter.

[Enter Sir Toby and Maria.]

10 SIR TOBY: Jove bless thee, Master Parson.
CLOWN: Bonos dies,† Sir Toby: for, as the old hermit of Prague, that never saw pen and ink, very wittily said to a niece of King Gorboduc,† 'That that is, is.' So I, being master parson, am Master Parson; for, what is 'that' but 'that'? and 'is' but
15 'is'?
SIR TOBY: To him,[6] Sir Topas.
CLOWN: What, ho, I say! Peace in this prison!
SIR TOBY: The knave counterfeits[7] well; a good knave.
MALVOLIO: *[From within.]* Who calls there?
20 CLOWN: Sir Topas the curate, who comes to visit Malvolio the lunatic.
MALVOLIO: Sir Topas, Sir Topas, good Sir Topas, go to my lady.
CLOWN: Out, hyperbolical[8] fiend! how vexest thou this man! talkest thou nothing but of ladies?
25 SIR TOBY: Well said, Master Parson.
MALVOLIO: Sir Topas, never was man thus wronged: good Sir Topas, do not think I am mad: they have laid me here in hideous darkness.
CLOWN: Fie, thou dishonest Satan! I call thee by the most mod-
30 est terms; for I am one of those gentle ones that will use

[1] *meanwhile*
[2] *disguise*
[3] *occupation (of a priest)*
[4] *host*
[5] *associates*
[6] *Go to him*
[7] *pretends*
[8] *exaggerated*

the devil himself with courtesy. Sayest thou that house[9] is dark?

MALVOLIO: As hell, Sir Topas.

CLOWN: Why, it hath bay windows transparent as barrica-
35 does,[10] and the clearstores[11] toward the south north are as lustrous as ebony; and yet complainest thou of obstruction?

MALVOLIO: I am not mad, Sir Topas: I say to you this house is dark.

40 CLOWN: Madman, thou errest: I say there is no darkness but ignorance; in which thou art more puzzled than the Egyptians in their fog.†

MALVOLIO: I say, this house is as dark as ignorance, though ignorance were as dark as hell;† and I say, there was never
45 man thus abused. I am no more mad than you are: make the trial of it in any constant question.[12]

CLOWN: What is the opinion of Pythagoras† concerning wild fowl?

MALVOLIO: That the soul of our grandam[13] might haply
50 inhabit a bird.

CLOWN: What thinkest thou of his opinion?

MALVOLIO: I think nobly of the soul, and no way approve his opinion.

55 CLOWN: Fare thee well. Remain thou still in darkness: thou shalt hold the opinion of Pythagoras ere I will allow of thy wits;[14] and fear to kill a woodcock, lest thou dispossess the soul of thy grandam. Fare thee well.

MALVOLIO: Sir Topas, Sir Topas!

60 SIR TOBY: My most exquisite Sir Topas!

CLOWN: Nay, I am for all waters.[15]

MARIA: Thou mightst have done this without thy beard and gown: he sees thee not.

SIR TOBY: To him[16] in thine own voice, and bring me word
65 how thou findest him: I would we were well rid of this knavery.[17] If he may be conveniently delivered,[18] I would he were; for I am now so far in offence with my niece that I cannot pursue with any safety this sport to the upshot.[19] Come by and by[20] to my chamber.

[Exeunt Sir Toby and Maria.]

[9] *room*

[10] *barricades*

[11] *high windows*

[12] *Test me by asking me some questions.*

[13] *grandmother*

[14] *before I grant that you are sane*

[15] *I am good at any occupation.*

[16] *Go to him*

[17] *villainy; bad behavior*

[18] *let out*

[19] *final outcome*

[20] *immediately*

70 CLOWN: *[Sings.]*

'Hey, Robin, jolly Robin,
Tell me how thy lady does.'†

MALVOLIO: Fool!

CLOWN: 'My lady is unkind, perdy.'[21]

75 MALVOLIO: Fool!

CLOWN: 'Alas, why is she so?'

MALVOLIO: Fool, I say!

CLOWN: 'She loves another.'
Who calls, ha?

80 MALVOLIO: Good fool, as ever thou wilt deserve well at my hand,[22] help me to a candle, and pen, ink, and paper; as I am a gentleman, I will live to be thankful to thee for't.

CLOWN: Master Malvolio?

MALVOLIO: Ay, good fool.

85 CLOWN: Alas, sir, how fell you besides[23] your five wits?†

MALVOLIO: Fool, there was never man so notoriously abused: I am as well in my wits, fool, as thou art.

CLOWN: But as well? then you are mad indeed, if you be no better in your wits than a fool.

90 MALVOLIO: They have here propertied[24] me; keep me in darkness, send ministers to me, asses, and do all they can to face me out of my wits.[25]

CLOWN: Advise you[26] what you say; the minister is here. Malvolio,† Malvolio, thy wits the heavens restore! endeavour

95 thyself to sleep, and leave thy vain bibble babble.[27]

MALVOLIO: Sir Topas!

CLOWN: Maintain no words with him,[28] good fellow. Who, I, sir? not I, sir. God be wi' you, good Sir Topas. Marry, amen. I will, sir, I will.

100 MALVOLIO: Fool, fool, fool, I say!

CLOWN: Alas, sir, be patient. What say you, sir? I am shent[29] for speaking to you.

MALVOLIO: Good fool, help me to some light and some paper: I tell thee I am as well in my wits as any man in Illyria.

105 CLOWN: Well-a-day[30] that you were, sir!

MALVOLIO: By this hand,[31] I am. Good fool, some ink, paper, and light; and convey what I will set down to my lady: it shall advantage thee[32] more than ever the bearing of letter did.[33]

CLOWN: I will help you to't. But tell me true, are you not mad

[21] *by God; certainly*

[22] *I will always treat you well (if you'll help me)*

[23] *how did you fall out of*

[24] *made me into a tool for their use*

[25] *make me look like I'm insane.*

[26] *Be careful*

[27] *idle talk; babble*

[28] *Do not speak with him*

[29] *blamed, reproved*

[30] *Alas*

[31] *I swear*

[32] *be advantageous to you*

[33] *more than any letter you've ever carried*

110 indeed? or do you but counterfeit?

MALVOLIO: Believe me, I am not; I tell thee true.

CLOWN: Nay, I'll ne'er believe a madman till I see his brains. I will fetch you light, and paper, and ink.

MALVOLIO: Fool, I'll requite[34] it in the highest degree: I prithee, be gone.

115 CLOWN: *[Sings.]*

'I am gone, sir,
And anon, sir,
I'll be with you again,
In a trice,[35]
120 Like to the old vice,
Your need to sustain;
Who with dagger of lath,[36]
In his rage and his wrath,
Cries ah, ha! to the devil:
125 Like a mad lad,
'Pare thy nails, dad.
Adieu, goodman devil.'† *[Exit.]*

[34] *repay*

[35] *moment*

[36] *piece of wood*

SCENE III
Olivia's Garden.

[Enter Sebastian.]

SEBASTIAN: This is the air; that is the glorious sun;
This pearl she gave me, I do feel't and see't;
And though 'tis wonder that enwraps me thus,
Yet 'tis not madness. Where's Antonio, then?
5 I could not find him at the Elephant:
Yet there he was; and there I found this credit,[1]
That he did range[2] the town to seek me out.
His counsel now might do me golden service;
For though my soul disputes well with my sense,
10 That this may be some error, but no madness,
Yet doth this accident and flood of fortune
So far exceed all instance, all discourse,[3]
That I am ready to distrust mine eyes
And wrangle with my reason that persuades me
15 To any other trust but that I am mad
Or else the lady's mad; yet, if 'twere so,

[1] *heard a report*

[2] *roam*

[3] *logic*

She could not sway[4] her house, command her followers,
Take and give back affairs and their dispatch[5]
With such a smooth, discreet, and stable bearing,
20 As I perceive she does: there's something in't
That is deceivable.[6] But here comes the lady.

[Enter Olivia and a Priest.]

OLIVIA: Blame not this haste of mine. If you mean well,
Now go with me and with this holy man
Into the chantry[7] by: there, before him
25 And underneath that consecrated roof,
Plight[8] me the full assurance of your faith,
That my most jealous and too doubtful soul
May live at peace. He shall conceal it
Whiles you are willing it shall come to note,
30 What time we will our celebration keep
According to my birth.† What do you say?

SEBASTIAN: I'll follow this good man, and go with you;
And, having sworn truth, ever will be true.

OLIVIA: Then lead the way, good father; and heavens so shine,
35 That they may fairly[9] note this act of mine!

[Exeunt.]

[4] *rule*

[5] *management*

[6] *deceptive, puzzling*

[7] *church*

[8] *Pledge*

[9] *fortunately*

ACT V

SCENE I
Before Olivia's house.

[Enter Clown and Fabian.]

FABIAN: Now, as thou lovest me, let me see his letter.
CLOWN: Good Master Fabian, grant me another request.
FABIAN: Anything.
CLOWN: Do not desire to see this letter.
5 FABIAN: This is to give a dog, and in recompense desire my dog again.†

[Enter Duke, Viola, and Attendants.]

DUKE ORSINO: Belong you to the Lady Olivia, friends?
CLOWN: Ay, sir; we are some of her trappings.[1]
DUKE ORSINO: I know thee well; how dost thou, my good fel-
10 low?
CLOWN: Truly, sir, the better for my foes and the worse for my friends.
DUKE ORSINO: Just the contrary; the better for thy friends.
CLOWN: No, sir, the worse.
15 DUKE ORSINO: How can that be?
CLOWN: Marry, sir, they praise me and make an ass of me; now my foes tell me plainly I am an ass: so that by my foes, sir, I profit in the knowledge of myself, and by my friends, I am abused: so that, conclusions to be as kisses, if your four nega-
20 tives make your two affirmatives,† why then, the worse for my friends and the better for my foes.
DUKE ORSINO: Why, this is excellent.

[1] *attendants*

CLOWN: By my troth, sir, no; though it please you to be one of my friends.

25 DUKE ORSINO: Thou shalt not be the worse for me: there's gold.

CLOWN: But that[2] it would be double-dealing,† sir, I would you could make it another.

[2]Except for the fact that

DUKE ORSINO: O, you give me ill counsel.

30 CLOWN: Put your grace in your pocket, sir, for this once, and let your flesh and blood obey it.†

DUKE ORSINO: Well, I will be so much a sinner to be a double-dealer: there's another.[3]

[3](coin)

CLOWN: Primo, secundo, tertio,† is a good play; and the old
35 saying is, the third pays for all:† the triplex,[4] sir, is a good tripping measure;[5] or the bells of Saint Bennet,† sir, may put you in mind; one, two, three.

[4]triple time

[5]dancing beat

DUKE ORSINO: You can fool no more money out of me at this throw:[6] if you will let your lady know I am here to speak
40 with her, and bring her along with you, it may awake my bounty further.

[6](of the dice)

CLOWN: Marry, sir, lullaby to your bounty till I come again. I go, sir; but I would not have you to think that my desire of having is the sin of covetousness: but, as you say, sir,
45 let your bounty take a nap, I will awake it anon.

[Exit Clown.]

[Enter Antonio and Officers.]

VIOLA: Here comes the man, sir, that did rescue me.

DUKE ORSINO: That face of his I do remember well;
Yet, when I saw it last, it was besmear'd
As black as Vulcan† in the smoke of war:
50 A bawbling[7] vessel was he captain of,
For shallow draught[8] and bulk unprizable;
With which such scathful grapple did he make
With the most noble bottom[9] of our fleet,
That very envy and the tongue of los
55 Cried fame and honour on him.† What's the matter?

[7]insignificant

[8]the amount of water a worthless boat displaces

[9]ship

FIRST OFFICER: Orsino, this is that Antonio
That took the Phoenix and her fraught[10] from Candy;†
And this is he that did the *Tiger* board,
When your young nephew Titus lost his leg:
60 Here in the streets, desperate of shame and state,[11]

[10]freight, cargo

[11]in a shameful condition

In private brabble[12] did we apprehend him.
VIOLA: He did me kindness, sir, drew on my side;[13]
But in conclusion put strange speech upon me.[14]
I know not what 'twas, but distraction.[15]
65 DUKE ORSINO: Notable pirate! thou salt-water thief!
What foolish boldness brought thee to their mercies,[16]
Whom thou, in terms so bloody and so dear,
Hast made thine enemies?
ANTONIO: Orsino, noble sir,
70 Be pleased that I shake off these names you give me:
Antonio never yet was thief or pirate,
Though, I confess, on base and ground enough,
Orsino's enemy. A witchcraft[17] drew me hither:
That most ingrateful boy there by your side,
75 From the rude sea's enraged and foamy mouth
Did I redeem;[18] a wreck past hope he was:
His life I gave him and did thereto add
My love, without retention or restraint,
All his in dedication; for his sake
80 Did I expose myself, pure[19] for his love,
Into the danger of this adverse town;
Drew to defend him when he was beset:[20]
Where being apprehended, his false cunning,
Not meaning to partake[21] with me in danger,
85 Taught him to face me out of his acquaintance,[22]
And grew a twenty years removed thing
While one would wink;† denied me mine own purse,
Which I had recommended to his use
Not half an hour before.
90 VIOLA: How can this be?
DUKE ORSINO: When came he to this town?
ANTONIO: Today, my lord; and for three months before,
No interim, not a minute's vacancy,[23]
Both day and night did we keep company.

[Enter Olivia and Attendants.]

95 DUKE ORSINO: Here comes the Countess: now heaven walks on earth.
But for thee, fellow; fellow, thy words are madness:
Three months this youth hath tended upon me;
But more of that anon. Take him aside.

[12]*brawl*

[13]*drew his sword to help me*

[14]*spoke strangely to me*

[15]*insanity*

[16]*brought you to your enemies' power*

[17]*irresistible charm; enchantment*

[18]*save*

[19]*purely*

[20]*in distress*

[21]*take part; share*

[22]*pretend not to know me*

[23]*empty time*

100 OLIVIA: What would my lord, but that he may not have,
Wherein Olivia may seem serviceable?
Cesario, you do not keep promise with me.
VIOLA: Madam—
DUKE ORSINO: Gracious Olivia,—
105 OLIVIA: What do you say, Cesario? Good my lord,—
VIOLA: My lord would speak; my duty hushes me.
OLIVIA: If it be aught[24] to the old tune, my lord,
It is as fat[25] and fulsome[26] to mine ear
As howling after music.
110 DUKE ORSINO: Still so cruel?
OLIVIA: Still so constant, lord.
DUKE ORSINO: What, to perverseness?[27] you uncivil lady,
To whose ingrate[28] and unauspicious[29] altars
My soul the faithfull'st offerings hath breathed out[30]
115 That e'er devotion tender'd![31] What shall I do?
OLIVIA: Even what it please my lord, that shall become him.[32]
DUKE ORSINO: Why should I not, had I the heart to do it,
Like to the Egyptian thief,† at point of death,
120 Kill what I love?—a savage jealousy
That sometime savours nobly.[33] But hear me this:
Since you to non-regardance cast my faith,[34]
And that I partly know the instrument
That screws[35] me from my true place in your favour,
125 Live you the marble-breasted tyrant still;
But this your minion,[36] whom I know you love,
And whom, by heaven I swear, I tender[37] dearly,
Him will I tear out of that cruel eye,[38]
Where he sits crowned in his master's sprite.[39]
130 Come, boy, with me; my thoughts are ripe in mischief:
I'll sacrifice the lamb that I do love,
To spite a raven's heart within a dove.
VIOLA: And I, most jocund,[40] apt, and willingly,
To do you rest,[41] a thousand deaths would die.
135 OLIVIA: Where goes Cesario?[42]
VIOLA: After him I love
More than I love these eyes, more than my life,
More, by all mores, than e'er I shall love wife.
If I do feign, you witnesses above
140 Punish my life for tainting of my love!
OLIVIA: Ah me, detested![43] how am I beguiled![44]

[24] *anything*
[25] *unnecessary, excessive*
[26] *offensive*
[27] *unkindness*
[28] *ungrateful*
[29] *unfavourable*
[30] *spoke*
[31] *offered, presented*
[32] *Whatever you want*
[33] *honourably*
[34] *neglect my love*
[35] *wrenches, forces*
[36] *favorite*
[37] *take care of; act kindly toward*
[38] *(Olivia's)*
[39] *despite his master (Orsino)*
[40] *lively, brisk*
[41] *to give you peace*
[42] *What is Cesario talking about?*
[43] *abominable!*
[44] *deceived, cheated*

VIOLA: Who does beguile you? who does do you wrong?
OLIVIA: Hast thou forgot thyself? Is it so long?[45]
Call forth the holy father. *[Exit an Attendant.]*
145 DUKE ORSINO: *[To Viola.]* Come, away!
OLIVIA: Whither, my lord? Cesario, husband, stay.
DUKE ORSINO: Husband?
OLIVIA: Ay, husband, can he that deny?[46]
DUKE ORSINO: *[To Viola.]* Her husband, sirrah?[47]
150 VIOLA: No, my lord, not I.
OLIVIA: Alas, it is the baseness[48] of thy fear
That makes thee strangle thy propriety:[49]
Fear not, Cesario, take thy fortunes up;[50]
Be that thou know'st thou art, and then thou art
155 As great as that thou fear'st.†

[Re-enter Attendant and Priest.]

O, welcome, father!
Father, I charge thee, by thy reverence,
Here to unfold,[51] though lately we intended
To keep in darkness what occasion now
160 Reveals before 'tis ripe, what thou dost know
Hath newly pass'd[52] between this youth and me.
PRIEST: A contract of eternal bond of love,
Confirm'd by mutual joinder[53] of your hands,
Attested by the holy close of lips,
165 Strengthen'd by interchangement[54] of your rings;
And all the ceremony of this compact
Seal'd in my function,[55] by my testimony:
Since when, my watch hath told me, toward my grave,
I have travelled but two hours.
170 DUKE ORSINO: *[To Viola.]* O thou dissembling cub![56] what wilt thou be,
When time hath sow'd a grizzle on thy case?[57]
Or will not else thy craft so quickly grow,
That thine own trip shall be thine overthrow?†
175 Farewell, and take her; but direct thy feet
Where thou and I henceforth may never meet.
VIOLA: My lord, I do protest—
OLIVIA: O, do not swear;
Hold little faith, though thou has too much fear.[58]

[Enter Sir Andrew.]

[45]*has it been so long?*

[46]*can he deny that?*

[47]*a disrespectful use of sin*

[48]*inferiority, low rank*

[49]*hide your identity*

[50]*accept your good luck*

[51]*reveal*

[52]*what you know has just happened*

[53]*joining*

[54]*exchange*

[55]*occupation, office*

[56]*lying little boy*

[57]*When time has put gray hair on you?*

[58]*Keep a little faith, even though you're afraid.*

180 SIR ANDREW: For the love of God, a surgeon! Send one presently to Sir Toby.

OLIVIA: What's the matter?

SIR ANDREW: He has broke my head across[59] and has given Sir Toby a bloody coxcomb[60] too: for the love of God, your
185 help! I had rather than forty pound I were at home.[61]

OLIVIA: Who has done this, Sir Andrew?

SIR ANDREW: The Count's gentleman, one Cesario: we took him for a coward, but he's the very devil incardinate.[62]

DUKE ORSINO: My gentleman, Cesario?

190 SIR ANDREW: 'Od's lifelings,[63] here he is! You broke my head for nothing; and that that I did, I was set on to do't[64] by Sir Toby.

VIOLA: Why do you speak to me? I never hurt you:
You drew your sword upon me without cause;
195 But I bespoke you fair,[65] and hurt you not.

SIR ANDREW: If a bloody coxcomb be a hurt, you have hurt me: I think you set nothing by[66] a bloody coxcomb.

[Enter Sir Toby, drunk, led by the Clown.]

Here comes Sir Toby halting;[67] you shall hear more: but if he had not been in drink[68] he would have tickled you[69]
200 othergates[70] than he did.

DUKE ORSINO: How now, gentleman? How is't with you?

SIR TOBY: That's all one:[71] he has hurt me, and there's the end on't. Sot, didst see Dick Surgeon, sot?[72]

CLOWN: O, he's drunk, Sir Toby, an hour agone; his eyes were
205 set[73] at eight i' the morning.

SIR TOBY: Then he's a rogue, and a passy-measure, or a pavin,† I hate a drunken rogue.

OLIVIA: Away with him! Who hath made this havoc with them?

210 SIR ANDREW: I'll help you, Sir Toby, because we'll be dressed[74] together.

SIR TOBY: Will you help an ass-head, and a coxcomb,[75] and a knave? a thin-faced knave, a gull?[76]

OLIVIA: Get him to bed, and let his hurt be look'd to.

[Exeunt Clown, Sir Toby, and Sir Andrew.]

[Enter Sebastian.]

[59] *wounded my head*

[60] *head*

[61] *I'd give up forty pounds to be at home.*

[62] *incarnate (in the flesh)*

[63] *God's little creatures (an exclamation)*

[64] *what I did, I was persuaded to do*

[65] *spoke to you kindly*

[66] *don't care about*

[67] *limping*

[68] *drunk*

[69] *served you right; made you pay*

[70] *other*

[71] *That doesn't matter*

[72] *Have you seen Dick the surgeon, fool?*

[73] *closed*

[74] *bandaged*

[75] *fool*

[76] *dupe, fool*

215 SEBASTIAN: I am sorry, madam, I have hurt your kinsman:
But, had it been the brother of my blood,
I must have done no less with wit and safety.[77]
You throw a strange regard upon me,[78] and by that
I do perceive it hath offended you:
220 Pardon me, sweet one, even for the vows
We made each other but so late ago.[79]
DUKE ORSINO: One face, one voice, one habit,[80] and two persons;
A natural perspective,[81] that is, and is not.
225 SEBASTIAN: Antonio! O my dear Antonio!
How have the hours rack'd[82] and tortured me,
Since I have lost thee!
ANTONIO: Sebastian are you?
SEBASTIAN: Fear'st thou[83] that, Antonio?
230 ANTONIO: How have you made division of yourself?
An apple, cleft[84] in two, is not more twin
Than these two creatures. Which is Sebastian?
OLIVIA: Most wonderful!
SEBASTIAN: Do I stand there? I never had a brother;
235 Nor can there be that deity in my nature,
Of here and everywhere. I had a sister,
Whom the blind waves and surges have devour'd.
Of charity,[85] what kin are you to me?
What countryman? what name? what parentage?
240 VIOLA: Of Messaline:† Sebastian was my father;
Such a Sebastian was my brother too:
So went he suited[86] to his watery tomb:
If spirits can assume both form and suit
You come to fright us.
245 SEBASTIAN: A spirit I am indeed;
But am in that dimension grossly clad
Which from the womb I did participate.[87]
Were you a woman, as the rest goes even,[88]
I should my tears let fall upon your cheek,
250 And say 'Thrice welcome, drowned Viola!'
VIOLA: My father had a mole upon his brow.
SEBASTIAN: And so had mine.
VIOLA: And died that day when Viola from her birth
Had numbered thirteen years.
255 SEBASTIAN: O, that record[89] is lively in my soul!
He finished, indeed, his mortal act

[77] *with thought for my own safety*

[78] *You give me a strange look*

[79] *so recently*

[80] *way of dressing*

[81] *an optical illusion*

[82] *tormented*

[83] *Do you doubt*

[84] *split*

[85] *in kindness*

[86] *dressed*

[87] *dressed the same as the day I was born*

[88] *and if all the other facts are correct*

[89] *memory*

That day that made my sister thirteen years.
VIOLA: If nothing lets[90] to make us happy both
But this my masculine usurp'd attire,
260 Do not embrace me till each circumstance
Of place, time, fortune, do cohere and jump[91]
That I am Viola: which to confirm,
I'll bring you to a captain in this town,
Where lie my maiden weeds;[92] by whose gentle help
265 I was preserved[93] to serve this noble Count;
All the occurrence of my fortune since
Hath been between this lady and this lord.
SEBASTIAN: *[To Olivia.]* So comes it, lady, you have been mistook:
270 But nature to her bias drew in that.[94]
You would have been contracted[95] to a maid;
Nor are you therein, by my life, deceived,
You are betroth'd both to a maid and man.
DUKE ORSINO: Be not amazed; right noble is his blood.
275 If this be so, as yet the glass seems true,
I shall have share in this most happy wreck:
[To Viola.] Boy, thou hast said to me a thousand times,
Thou never shouldst love woman like to me.[96]
VIOLA: And all those sayings will I overswear;[97]
280 And all those swearings keep as true in soul
As doth that orbed continent the fire[98]
That severs day from night.
DUKE ORSINO: Give me thy hand;
And let me see thee in thy woman's weeds.
285 VIOLA: The captain that did bring me first on shore
Hath my maid's garments: he upon some action,[99]
Is now in durance,[100] at Malvolio's suit,[101]
A gentleman, and follower of my lady's.
OLIVIA: He shall enlarge him:[102] fetch Malvolio hither:
290 And yet, alas, now I remember me,
They say, poor gentleman, he's much distract.[103]

[Re-enter Clown, with a letter.]
A most extracting frenzy of mine own
From my remembrance clearly banish'd his.[104]
How does he, sirrah?
295 CLOWN: Truly, madam, he holds Belzebub[105] at the stave's end[106] as well as a man in his case may do: he has here

[90] *prevents*
[91] *agree*
[92] *female clothes*
[93] *saved*
[94] *corrected the course of your mistake*
[95] *engaged*
[96] *like you love me*
[97] *swear again*
[98] *As the sun keeps its fire*
[99] *legality*
[100] *imprisoned*
[101] *because of Malvolio's lawsuit*
[102] *free him*
[103] *crazy*
[104] *other thoughts of mine made me forget about Malvolio*
[105] *the devil*
[106] *end of a stick*

writ a letter to you; I should have given it you today morning, but as a madman's epistles are no gospels, so it skills not much[107] when they are delivered.

300 OLIVIA: Open't, and read it.

CLOWN: Look then to be well edified when the fool delivers the madman. *[Reads]* 'By the Lord, madam,'—

OLIVIA: How now! art thou mad?

CLOWN: No, madam, I do but read madness: an your ladyship

305 will have it as it ought to be, you must allow Vox.†

OLIVIA: Prithee, read i' thy right wits.[108]

CLOWN: So I do, madonna; but to read his right wits is to read thus; therefore perpend,[109] my princess, and give ear.

OLIVIA: *[To Fabian.]* Read it you, sirrah.

310 FABIAN: *[Reads]*

'By the Lord, madam, you wrong me, and the world shall know it: though you have put me into darkness and given your drunken cousin rule over me, yet have I the benefit of my senses as well as your ladyship. I have your own letter that induced

315 me to the semblance I put on; with the which[110] I doubt not but to do myself much right or you much shame. Think of me as you please. I leave my duty a little unthought of,[111] and speak out of my injury.

The madly-used Malvolio.'

OLIVIA: Did he write this?

320 CLOWN: Ay, madam.

DUKE ORSINO: This savours not much of distraction.[112]

OLIVIA: See him deliver'd,[113] Fabian; bring him hither.

[Exit Fabian.]

My lord so please you, these things further thought on,[114]
To think me as well a sister as a wife,†

325 One day shall crown the alliance on't,[115] so please you,
Here at my house and at my proper cost.[116]

DUKE ORSINO: Madam, I am most apt to embrace your offer.
[To Viola] Your master quits you;[117] and, for your service done him,

330 So much against the mettle of your sex,[118]
So far beneath your soft and tender breeding,
And since you call'd me master for so long,
Here is my hand: you shall from this time be
You master's mistress.

335 OLIVIA: A sister! you are she.

[107] *it doesn't matter too much*

[108] *normally*

[109] *consider*

[110] *with which*

[111] *I'll ignore my duty right now*

[112] *This doesn't seem like insanity.*

[113] *set free*

[114] *once you have thought more about this*

[115] *we'll all (both couples) be married on the same day*

[116] *at my expense*

[117] *releases*

[118] *character of your gender*

[Re-enter Fabian with Malvolio.]

DUKE ORSINO: Is this the madman?
OLIVIA: Ay, my lord, this same;
How now, Malvolio?
MALVOLIO: Madam, you have done me wrong,
340 Notorious wrong.
OLIVIA: Have I, Malvolio? no.
MALVOLIO: Lady, you have. Pray you, peruse that letter.
You must not now deny it is your hand:
Write from it, if you can, in hand or phrase;
345 Or say 'tis not your seal, not your invention:[119]
You can say none of this: well, grant it then,
And tell me, in the modesty of honour,[120]
Why you have given me such clear lights of favour;[121]
Bade me come smiling and cross-garter'd to you;
350 To put on yellow stockings, and to frown
Upon Sir Toby and the lighter[122] people:
And, acting this in an obedient hope,
Why have you suffer'd me to be imprison'd,
Kept in a dark house, visited by the priest,
355 And made the most notorious geck[123] and gull
That e'er invention played on? tell me why.
OLIVIA: Alas, Malvolio, this is not my writing,
Though, I confess, much like the character[124]
But out of question,[125] 'tis Maria's hand.
360 And now I do bethink me, it was she
First told me thou wast mad; then camest in smiling,
And in such forms which here were presupposed
Upon thee in the letter.[126] Prithee, be content:
This practice hath most shrewdly pass'd upon thee;[127]
365 But, when we know the grounds and authors of it,
Thou shalt be both the plaintiff and the judge
Of thine own cause.
FABIAN: Good madam, hear me speak;
And let no quarrel, nor no brawl to come
370 Taint the condition of this present hour,[128]
Which I have wonder'd[129] at. In hope it shall not,
Most freely I confess, myself and Toby
Set this device against Malvolio here,
Upon some stubborn and uncourteous parts[130]
375 We had conceived against him: Maria writ

[119] *thought, idea*

[120] *with consideration for your own honor*

[121] *signals that you like me*

[122] *inferior*

[123] *fool*

[124] *style*

[125] *there is no question*

[126] *And acting in the way the letter told you to act*

[127] *was maliciously played on you*

[128] *stain the quality of this moment*

[129] *marvelled*

[130] *characteristics*

The letter at Sir Toby's great importance;[131]
In recompense whereof he hath married her.
How with a sportful malice it was follow'd
May rather pluck on[132] laughter than revenge;
380 If that the injuries be justly weigh'd
That have on both sides past.[133]

OLIVIA: *[To Malvolio.]* Alas, poor fool, how have they baffled thee!

CLOWN: Why, 'some are born great, some achieve greatness, and
385 some have greatness thrown upon them.' I was one, sir, in this interlude: one Sir Topas, sir; but that's all one. 'By the Lord, fool, I am not mad.' But do you remember? 'Madam, why laugh you at such a barren rascal? An you smile not, he's gagged:' and thus the whirligig[134] of time brings in his
390 revenges.

MALVOLIO: I'll be revenged on the whole pack of you. *[Exit.]*

OLIVIA: He hath been most notoriously abus'd.

DUKE ORSINO: Pursue him, and entreat him to a peace:[135]
He hath not told us of the captain yet:†
395 When that is known and golden time convents,[136]
A solemn combination shall be made
Of our dear souls. Meantime, sweet sister,
We will not part from hence. Cesario, come:
For so you shall be, while you are a man;
400 But when in other habits you are seen,
Orsino's mistress, and his fancy's queen.† *[Exeunt.]*

CLOWN: *[Sings]*

When that I was and a little tiny boy,
With hey, ho, the wind and the rain,
A foolish thing was but a toy,
For the rain it raineth every day.†
405 But when I came to man's estate,
With hey, ho, the wind and the rain,
'Gainst knave and thief men shut their gate,
For the rain it raineth every day.
But when I came, alas, to wive,
410 With hey, ho, the wind and the rain,
By swaggering could I never thrive,
For the rain it raineth every day.
But when I came unto my beds,
With hey, ho, the wind and the rain,
With toss-pots still had drunken heads,[137]

[131] *urgent request*

[132] *Let us rather draw on*

[133] *Since both sides have been injured equally.*

[134] *spinning top*

[135] *beg him to calm down*

[136] *comes together*

[137] *drunkards that were still drunk*

415 For the rain it raineth every day.
A great while ago the world begun,
With hey, ho, the wind and the rain,
But that's all one,[138] our play is done,
And we'll strive to please you every day.

[138] *that doesn't matter*

[Exit.]

Glossary

Act I, Scene I

"If music be the food of love…and so die." – Orsino is saying that since music is the food of love, he wants it to continue playing so his appetite for love will be filled so much that it will eventually die. This opening line reveals a lot about Orsino's character and also about one of the themes of the play. Orsino is melodramatic about his love for Olivia, as the above line illustrates. Throughout the play, it seems as though he is more in love with the *idea* of being in love than with Olivia herself. The line also establishes the theme of love as a sickness or a force that strikes people without warning or invitation. Both Orsino and Olivia are self-involved people who actually enjoy the suffering and drama that being in love brings.

"O spirit of love!…low price…" – Orsino means that love is so great that it has the capacity of the sea. However, anything that falls into love (as if love is a great ocean) eventually loses its value, no matter how priceless it had been before. Just as things are transformed into insignificance by the sea, they are also swallowed up and made unimportant by love.

"…so full of shapes is fancy…high fantastical." – Orsino means that love (*fancy*) is deceptive, can take many forms, and can be more about fantasy than about reality. Instead of being truly in love, Orsino seems to be a victim of the *fantasy* of love.

"Why, so I do, the noblest that I have…" – Curio has just asked Orsino about hunting the hart, a male deer. Orsino, however, gives the word a double meaning. By "the noblest that I have," he refers to both a *hart* and a *heart* (Olivia's).

"That instant was I turn'd into a hart…pursue me." – Orsino is referring to the ancient Greek myth of Actaeon and Artemis. Actaeon was out hunting when he saw the naked Artemis bathing. As punishment for watching her, she turned him into a deer. Actaeon was then chased and torn to pieces by his own hounds. In this metaphor, Orsino compares himself to Actaeon and compares his desires to the destructive hounds.

"…till seven years' heat…" – until seven years of the sun's course across the sky

"…she will veiled walk…eye-offending brine…" – Valentine is explaining that Olivia wears a veil and stays in her room all day mourning for her dead brother. The "eye-offending brine" refers to tears that she cries at least once a day.

"the rich golden shaft" – a reference to the golden arrow of Cupid, the Roman god of love

"liver, brain, and heart" – While Elizabethans considered the brain the center of thought, both the liver and the heart were believed to be the locations of love and emotion.

Act I, Scene II

Illyria – an ancient country on the Adriatic Sea, somewhere near present-day Albania

Elysium – the only good part of Hades, the underworld; this is the Greek equivalent of paradise, where righteous people were supposed to find happiness after they died. It is sometimes referred to as the Elysian Fields or Plains.

"Arion on the dolphin's back" – The captain is referring to the story of Arion, a Greek poet living in the 7th century BC, who was supposedly saved from drowning by a dolphin. According to legend, Arion was threatened by pirates. Before throwing him overboard, the pirates allowed him to sing one last song. The dolphin was charmed by Arion's voice and carried him away to safety.

"O that I served...my estate is!" – In this passage, Viola expresses her wish to remain anonymous and unknown until she decides to divulge her true identity as a noblewoman.

"And though that nature...pollution..." – This metaphor expresses the idea that looks can be deceiving and that an outwardly virtuous person might be immoral inside.

"Conceal me what I am...form of my intent." – Viola has decided to disguise herself as a young man in order to be hired as a servant in Orsino's household. This passage sets up one of the main conflicts of the play.

eunuch – Eunuchs were males who had been castrated, which resulted in the stunting of certain growth characteristics, such as growing beards or the deepening of the voice. Eunuchs were generally employed as servants to royalty or as guardians of harems because they were believed to be less threatening than other men. Viola cleverly realizes that she may be able to get away with her disguise more easily if people believe she is a eunuch.

Act I, Scene III

Sir Toby Belch – Shakespeare gives Sir Toby a deliberately amusing name. Sir Toby Belch is a drunkard and a glutton, who is rude and crude throughout the play.

cousin – In Shakespeare's time, the word *cousin* could refer to almost any relation.

"...let her except, before excepted." – Sir Toby apparently means, "let her object to my behavior; it doesn't change anything." The line itself is a play on a common Latin legal term used during Elizabethan times, *exceptis excipiendis*. The term meant "allowing for certain exceptions." It was mainly used in lease agreements to stipulate that certain conditions that existed before the signing of the lease would still be allowed. It seems fitting for Sir Toby, since he is able to misbehave without being kicked out of the house simply because he is Olivia's relative.

Sir Andrew Aguecheek – another humorous name; *ague* refers to a fever combined with fits of shivering.

ducats – gold coins used throughout Europe during the time of the play

viol-de-gamboys – a musical instrument similar to the cello

"almost natural" – This is a pun on the word *natural*. In Shakespearean times, *natural* was a slang term for *idiot*.

"turn o' the toe like a parish-top" – Parishes were townships that were formed around a central church. The parish top was a large top that stood in the village square, which citizens could spin for entertainment.

"Castiliano vulgo!" – [*Spanish*] Castilian people; it seems as though Sir Toby uses this expression to quiet Maria. Some critics have suggested that, because the Castilian people had a reputation for politeness, Sir Toby is using the phrase as a command for Maria to be polite to Sir Andrew.

"Good Mistress Accost" – Sir Andrew doesn't understand what is happening and thinks Maria's name is *Accost*.

buttery-bar – a room, usually in the cellar where liquor and other provisions were stored

"It's dry, sir." – Maria is playing with Sir Andrew regarding the word *dry*. In Shakespeare's time, a person with a dry hand was believed to be impotent or disinterested in love.

"a cup of canary" – a type of wine from the Canary Islands

"Methinks sometimes...does harm to my wit." – By *Christian*, Sir Andrew means simply, the average man. During Elizabethan times, many people thought that eating too much beef was bad for the brain.

bear-baiting – a popular amusement during Elizabethan times in which a bear was chained up and dogs were set loose to attack the bear

"Then hadst thou had an excellent...spin it off." – Sir Toby engages in sexual puns, but Aguecheek does not understand the reference to syphilis ("spin it off") nor to the negative comments about his appearance ("hangs like flax on a distaff").

"And I can cut the mutton to't." – Sir Toby is punning on the word *caper*, which has just been spoken by Sir Andrew. While a caper is a type of dance, it is also a type of salted berry eaten with mutton.

Mistress Mall – Many critics have tried to find out who Mistress Mall was, if indeed it is an actual individual. Unfortunately, there is no definitive answer regarding the reference; it is possible the name means "any woman."

sink-a-pace – Sir Toby is punning on the word *cinque pace* (five-steps), a French dance.

"Taurus? that's sides and heart." – Astrological signs were thought to correspond to certain parts of the body.

Act I, Scene IV

"Diana's lip" – a reference to the goddess of the hunt from ancient Roman mythology

constellation – Although a constellation is a grouping of stars, Duke Orsino is referring to Viola/Cesario's personal characteristics. It was believed that a person's character was determined by the constellation associated with his or her birth date.

"Whoe'er I woo, myself would be his wife." – With this statement, Viola makes it clear that she has fallen in love with Orsino. The love triangle that surrounds the plot is now completely set up. Orsino is in love with Olivia, while Olivia is falling for Cesario, who is Viola in disguise. Viola now confesses that she is in love with Orsino. Making this triangle even more problematic is the fact that both Olivia and Orsino believe that Viola is a man.

Act I, Scene V

"...he that is well hanged...fear no colours." – Feste is punning on the word *collars*, which of course sounds like *colours*. (See note: "In the wars" below.)

"In the wars" – Maria points out the origin of the phrase "fear no colours." The word *colours* was used to describe military flags displayed on the battlefield.

"Well, God give them...use their talents." – Feste is saying that intelligent people utilize wisdom, but those without intelligence must utilize talent. He seems to put himself in the latter category. However, Feste is highly intelligent, as well as talented, as were most professional fools at this time.

"let summer bear it out" – Feste means that if he does get kicked out of Olivia's house, the fact that it is summertime will make his eviction less troublesome.

"That if one break...your gaskins fall." – Maria is punning on the word *point*, which refers to the small hooks used to hold up trousers—*gaskins*.

"...if Sir Toby would leave drinking...as any in Illyria." – "If Sir Toby would quit drinking, he would do well to marry you, one of the cleverest women in Illyria."

"Wit, an't be thy will, put me into good fooling!" – "Wit, if it be your will, help me to be clever and amusing." Feste is addressing the abstract concept of wit. This literary device is called an *apostrophe*. Not to be confused with the punctuation mark, this kind of apostrophe is seen whenever a character speaks directly to an object or an abstract idea.

Quinapalus – This is a fictitious philosopher invented by Feste.

"Any thing that's mended...patched with virtue." – "Anything that has been mended has been patched. A virtuous person who goes astray is patched with sin, while a sinful person who does a virtuous thing is patched with virtue." Feste means that no one is completely sinful or completely virtuous. Instead, all people have a mixture of virtue and sin within them.

"As there is no true cuckold...beauty's a flower..." – "Just as disaster is the worst kind of betrayal, it is also true that beauty does not last." Feste is stating that all men are married to luck, and when a man's luck betrays him (as it does whenever calamity strikes) he has been made a cuckold (a man betrayed by his wife). In comparing beauty to a flower, he means that beauty, like the flower, is not permanent. It blooms for a short time and then dies.

"'*Cucullus non facit monachum*...motley in my brain." – "The cowl does not make the monk." In other words, the costume a person wears has no bearing on what kind of person he or she really is. "Motley" refers to the multicolored scraps of cloth that most clown costumes were made of.

"my mouse of virtue" – The word *mouse* was often used as a term of endearment.

Malvolio – As he did with "Toby Belch" and "Andrew Aguecheek," Shakespeare again chooses a name that describes one of his characters. In Italian, *Mal volio* can be translated to "ill will." This is fitting, since Malvolio will be the main antagonist for the other characters in the play.

zanies – A zany was a lesser clown whose job was to imitate a professional clown.

"O, you are sick of self-love, Malvolio..." – Malvolio is extremely self-centered and self-righteous. These traits allow for him to become the victim of Sir Toby's malicious scheme later on in the play.

"take those things for bird-bolts...nothing but reprove." – Bird-bolts were small arrows used for shooting birds. Olivia is telling Malvolio that he should take Feste's insults less seriously. Olivia also explains that a professional fool can never be guilty of slander since part of the fool's job is to insult people.

"Now Mercury endue thee with leasing" – "Now Mercury supplies you with the ability to lie." The ancient Roman god Mercury was believed to be crafty and deceptive.

Jove – the ancient Roman god, Jupiter

pia mater – the membrane covering the brain

"a plague o' these pickle-herring!" – Sir Toby has just belched and is cursing the pickled herring that he had eaten.

"Lechery! I defy lechery." – Whether he does it intentionally or not, Sir Toby mistakes the word *lethargy* (laziness) for the word *lechery* (lewdness). This is an example of a malapropism.

"Well, it's all one." – "It makes no difference."

"one draught above heat" – one drink more than the amount thought necessary to heat the body

sheriff's post – a reference to the elaborately carved posts, which were erected in front of the doors of town officials

"...as a squash is before...between boy and man." – A squash is an unripe pea pod; a codling is an unripe apple. Standing water refers to the tide just before it turns, when the water seems to stand still. Malvolio uses these metaphors to describe the appearance of Viola/Cesario, indicating her age.

"...if you are she...yours to reserve." – "If you are the lady of the house, you assume your role falsely, because what is yours to give (meaning, your hand in marriage) is not yours to keep." Viola means that Olivia should be married.

"...'tis not that time of moon...so skipping a dialogue." – "I am not crazy enough to be a part of this wayward and thoughtless dialogue." Some people believed that the moon could cause madness.

"Will you hoist sail, sir? here lies your way." – "Will you please leave? Here is the way out." Note the sailing imagery.

"No, good swabber…sweet lady." – Viola continues Maria's imagery of sailors on a ship. A *swabber* is a person who cleans the deck of a ship. "To hull" means to stop sailing and float for a while. Viola also ironically refers to Maria, who is small in stature, as a "giant" who guards Olivia.

"Olivia: Tell me your mind. / Viola: I am a messenger." – Depending on what version of *Twelfth Night* you are using, these lines appear differently. Some versions have Viola speaking both lines. It seems more appropriate, however, to have Olivia speak "Tell me your mind." This line indicates that she wants to get to know Viola/Cesario better. Olivia is beginning to show romantic feelings for Cesario and, therefore, desires him to talk with her more. Viola, keeping the relationship professional, states plainly that she is the messenger and, therefore, should not speak too much.

"I hold the olive…peace as matter." – "I ask for peace; my words are as peaceful as they are meaningful."

"Look you, sir…Is't not well done?" – "Look at me. This is how I looked just a minute ago, before I put on my veil. Isn't my face quite beautiful?"

"'Tis in grain" – *Grain* refers to a type of permanent dye. Olivia means that her face is naturally beautiful and that she has no need to wear makeup.

"Lady, you are the cruell'st…no copy." – "Lady, you are the cruelest woman alive if you insist on wearing your veil forever and letting no one see your beauty."

"Make me a willow cabin at your gate…" – The willow tree was a symbol of sorrow for unreturned love.

"spend this for me" – Olivia is handing Viola some money.

"Love make his heart of flint…contempt!" – "I hope the person you fall in love with has a heart as hard as flint. I hope your own passion will be despised, just as you despise Orsino's passion."

"Unless the master were the man." – "If only Duke Orsino were Cesario." Olivia is falling in love with Cesario.

"Even so quickly…creep in at mine eyes." – In the same way that Orsino likened love to an illness in Scene I, Olivia likens it to a plague in this passage. This statement also attests to the random force of love, which seems to be uncontrollable; it imposes itself on people when they least expect it.

"The County's man: he left this ring behind him…" – By "the County's man," Olivia simply means "the Count's man." The ring is a token of Olivia's love for Cesario.

"Mine eye too great a flatterer…and be this so." – Olivia means that she has fallen for Cesario's beauty, but that her intellect is at odds with this. This line emphasizes the theme of love as a form of madness. The last two lines underscore the belief that fate determines everything and that people have no real control over events.

Act II, Scene I

"My stars shine darkly...distemper yours..." – Sebastian believes that the stars predict a bad future for him. He advises Antonio to leave him so that the bad luck will not rub off on Antonio as well.

"...if the heavens had been pleased...so ended!" – Sebastian is expressing his wish that he and his twin sister could have died together as well.

"If you will not murder...be your servant." – "Please do not kill me by leaving me. Let me go with you and be your servant instead." Much has been made of the level of affection that Antonio feels for Sebastian. Some critics suggest that Antonio is actually in love with Sebastian, but many also believe that the two men simply have a very strong friendship. Such deeply felt friendships between men were not unusual during Shakespeare's time.

Act II, Scene II

"She took the ring of me: I'll none of it." – "She took the ring from me. I refuse to take it back." Viola decides to play along with Olivia's deception, letting Malvolio believe that she (as Cesario) did indeed leave a ring with Olivia. In truth, it is Olivia who is using Malvolio to deliver the ring as a gift to Cesario.

"Disguise, I see...to set their forms!" – Some critics believe that the passage alludes to the devil disguising himself as a serpent in order to seduce Eve.

"O time! thou must untangle...for me to untie!" – This is another reference to the idea that people have no control over the situations in which they find themselves. Instead, it is fate that controls things. The passage also alludes to the fact that, for the audience, time *will* untangle the knot before the play's end.

Act II, Scene III

"diluculo surgere" – [*Latin*] "to get up at dawn"; the full phrase is *diluculo surgere saluberrimum est*, which means "to get up at dawn is most healthful."

the four elements – earth, air, fire, and water

"did you never see the picture of 'we three'?" – Feste is referring to a popular sign that was seen in front of Elizabethan taverns. The phrase "We three loggerheads be" was painted underneath a picture of two fools. (*Loggerhead* refers to a dolt or a fool.) The person reading the sign became the third fool.

"Pigrogromitus, of the Vapians...Queubus..." – These are all terms made up by Sir Andrew, which are intended to sound like astrological terms.

"I did impeticos...no bottle-ale houses." – Critics do not entirely agree on what Feste means to say, although it is most likely a bit of nonsense he is using in order to amuse Sir Andrew and Sir Toby. Aguecheek, in his response, pretends to understand the words completely, so the wordplay has worked. It might be translated to something like this: "I did pocket the tip you gave me, for Malvolio's nose is not a whip handle; my lady is pure, and the Myrmidons aren't cheap taverns." In ancient Greek mythology, Myrmidons were the faithful followers of Achilles. However, in this context, it seems that *Myrmidons* refers to the name of a tavern.

"a catch that will draw…out of one weaver" – Since weavers were well known to be good singers, Sir Toby means that the men should sing as loudly and enthusiastically as weavers.

"My lady's a Cataian…and 'Three merry men be we.'" – *Cataian* was a derogatory term for a Chinese person. *Peg-a-Ramsey* refers to a song titled "Bonny Peggy Ramsey" in which the heroine is a pretty girl who is also quite crude and immoral. It appears that Sir Toby is speaking ironically of Malvolio, since Malvolio's character is completely opposite that of the song's heroine. "Three merry men be we" refers to a song that was popular during the time in which the play was written.

"'There dwelt a man in Babylon, lady, lady.'" – a reference to an old English ballad titled "The Constancy of Susanna"

"'Farewell, dear heart, since I must needs be gone.'" – a reference to another old English ballad titled "Corydon's Farewell to Phyllis"; Sir Toby and Feste sing the song back and forth to each other for the next several lines.

"Art any more than…no more cakes and ale?" – "You're nothing more than a server. Do you think that simply because you're virtuous, no one else should be able to enjoy any more food?" Sir Toby speaks these lines to Malvolio. This passage illuminates the character of Malvolio and the fact that, throughout the play, Malvolio is the prudish antagonist who always tries to ruin everyone's fun.

"ginger shall be hot i' the mouth" – Ginger was thought to reduce the effects of alcohol when it was used to flavor drinks.

"Go sir, rub your chain with crumbs." – In his duty of household steward, Malvolio carries a set of keys on a chain with him. Sir Toby is insulting Malvolio by proposing that Malvolio rub his chain with crumbs. Since crumbs are bits of wasted bread, Sir Toby is essentially reminding Malvolio of his lower class status.

"Go shake your ears." – "You are an ass." The imagery is that of an ass (or donkey) shaking its ears.

Puritan – By the word *Puritan*, Maria simply means that Malvolio is *like* a Puritan, overly virtuous and too strict about everything. Sir Andrew, however, thinks she means that Malvolio is an actual adherent to the Puritan faith. Puritanism was a Protestant movement in England during the 16th and 17th centuries. Puritans believed that the Church of England needed to be reformed, or purified. Sir Andrew, being a member of the Church of England, would intensely dislike anyone described as a Puritan.

"I will plant you two…find the letter" – Maria says that she will have Sir Andrew and Sir Toby hide so that they may witness the joke she will soon play on Malvolio. Interestingly, she says that Feste will be the third witness. However, the third witness happens to be Fabian and not Feste. Critics suggest this may have been an original mistake of Shakespeare's or a mistake that happened during revisions of the play.

Penthesilea – In ancient Greek mythology, Penthesilia was queen of the Amazons, a race of aggressive warrior women. This is one of several ironic references to Maria's small stature.

"call me cut" – *Cut* refers to a horse whose tail has been clipped short. It is used as a term of contempt.

Act II, Scene IV

"A little, by your favour." – *Favour* has a double meaning in this line. The phrase "by your favour" means "by your allowance" or "if you please." However, the word *favour* can also mean "face" or "appearance" as it does in the previous line when Duke Orsino uses it. Viola is telling Orsino that she loves *his* face, but she deliberately uses the ambiguous word *favour* so that Orsino thinks she merely means "if you please."

"let still the woman...women's are." – Orsino is saying that a woman should marry an older man, so that he will not tire of her as easily as a younger man will. He explains his belief that men are more fickle than women when it comes to love.

cypress – In this sense, *cypress* refers to a coffin made out of the wood of the cypress tree, commonly associated with mourning.

yew – another tree that is associated with mourning

"...taffeta, thy mind...very opal." – Taffeta is a thin, silk-like material that changes color depending on the way it reflects light, and an opal is a gemstone that is composed of many colors. Note that the sea, the other image in the speech, is also very changeable. Basically, Feste is telling Orsino that to have a fickle nature, one that changes, is to have nothing of substance.

"There is no woman's sides...I owe Olivia." – Orsino is saying that women cannot love as deeply as men can. He believes that a woman's appetite for love is easily satisfied and that eventually the woman becomes sick and tired of love. On the other hand, *his* appetite for love is bottomless like the sea. This passage firmly supports the fact that Orsino is so overly dramatic about his own feelings of love that he seems quite shallow and self-centered. He also contradicts himself. Just a few lines earlier, he was telling Cesario that men are more fickle than women are regarding love and that they need to marry younger women so they don't tire of them so quickly. Orsino regards himself as an authority on love, but it is easy to see that he does not understand it at all.

"My father...your lordship." – Viola makes another cleverly ambiguous statement regarding her identity and her feelings for Orsino.

"She sat like patience...at grief." – During Shakespeare's time, the figure representing the concept of patience was often seen on gravestones.

Act II, Scene V

"my nettle of India" – It was believed that India was rich in gold, so the reference means "my golden one."

"the trout that must be caught with tickling" – It was believed that one could induce a trance-like state in a trout by tickling its underbelly. Malvolio will be "tickled" through flattery.

"Contemplation...advanced plumes!" – Malvolio is likened to a male turkey, a bird that was representative of foolish pride and arrogance.

"To be Count Malvolio!" – Here Malvolio reveals his ambition to marry Olivia and rise above his class. This characteristic of Malvolio seems to be the feature that makes him so despised by Sir Toby and the others. In fact, Malvolio's character plays out one of the major themes of the play—the folly of ambition. In Elizabethan times, it was foolish to think that one could rise up out of the social class into which one had been born.

"...the lady of the Strachy...the wardrobe." – There is no agreement regarding the identity of "the lady of the Strachy," nor whether the words even refer to an actual person. In any case, Malvolio refers to this couple to convince himself that one can marry above one's class.

Jezebel – In the Old Testament, Jezebel is the evil and scheming wife of Ahab. It seems that Sir Andrew is either using her name as a curse or he is referring to Malvolio's scheming character.

"Though our silence...with cars..." – This is a reference to a method of torture in which the person to be tortured was tied to two carts. Horses pulled the two carts in opposite directions and the person was essentially pulled apart.

"these be her very...great P's." – Some scholars believe that Shakespeare makes a vulgar pun with these lines, however, it is not certain that this is the case.

"By your leave...she uses to seal..." – Malvolio asks the wax for permission before he unseals the letter. Letters were usually sealed with wax, and people had their own personal stamps that they used to make an impression in the wax. Olivia's stamp apparently depicts Lucrece (or Lucretia), a virtuous woman in Roman legend who was raped and then committed suicide.

"Sowter will cry...as rank as a fox." – *Sowter* refers to a cobbler or a shoemaker and, in this case, is also the name of the dog to which Malvolio is being compared. The line can be translated to the following: "The dog will follow the scent, even though the smell of deception should be as obvious as the scent of a fox."

"the cur is excellent at faults" – In hunting, faults are areas where the scent has been lost. Faults are also defects or imperfections, of which Malvolio is believed to have many.

"Remember who commended...cross-gartered..." – During Elizabethan times, men wore garters to hold up their stockings. To cross-garter was to unconventionally cross the garters both above and below the knee. Since Olivia hates the style of cross-gartering, Malvolio will look like a fool to her.

"the Sophy" – the king of Persia

"Wilt thou set thy foot o' my neck?" – Sir Toby is telling Maria that she has conquered him with her impressive wit. The imagery is of a conqueror standing over a victim with a foot on the victim's neck.

"Like aqua-vitae with a midwife." – "Like strong alcohol with a midwife." While a midwife refers to a woman who helps other women during childbirth, in Shakespeare's time, the term *midwife* was also used as a derogatory term for an old woman. Sir Toby apparently means that the deception works upon Malvolio in the same way that whiskey works on an old woman.

"the gates of Tartar" – Tartar is another word for hell. Sir Toby means "the gates of hell."

Act III, Scene I

"the king lies…by the church." – Viola is continuing the wordplay that Feste started. While Feste was punning on the phrase "to live by," Viola puns on the phrases "to lie by" and "to stand by."

"But indeed words…disgraced them." – Feste is lamenting the fact that formal contracts (or bonds) are now used in place of verbal agreements. A person's word does not mean as much as it once did.

"I would play…to this Troilus." – Troilus and Cressida were legendary lovers who were brought together by Cressida's uncle Pandarus, from whom we get the verb *to pander*. Feste is essentially saying that he would like to be Pandarus so that he could bring a female coin to the male coin.

"Cressida was a beggar" – In later versions of the story of Troilus and Cressida, she contracts leprosy and dies as a beggar.

"…like the haggard, check at every feather…" – "like the untrained hawk stops in mid-pursuit to go after another prey…"

"The matter, I hope…taint their wit." – Notice how Shakespeare changes from prose to verse and back again throughout the text. In many instances, language and the style of speaking (prose and verse) are directly correlated with a character's social ranking. Nobility and aristocracy will typically speak in verse, whereas servants and members of the lower classes will speak in prose.

The fact that Viola is an aristocrat disguised as a servant explains why she will, sometimes suddenly, switch from speaking in prose to verse. In this specific instance, Viola is coming out of character (from Cesario) after the clown exits, which explains her use of verse here, rather than prose. Later, however, pay attention to this fact when Viola is speaking to Olivia as Cesario.

"'Odours,' 'pregnant'…all three ready." – It seems that Sir Andrew is impressed with Viola's words and is trying to commit them to memory so that he can use them later himself.

"'Twas never merry…compliment…" – "The world isn't what it used to be. It's a sad state of affairs when a lowly pretense of humility passes for a compliment."

"But, would you undertake...the spheres." – It was believed that the universe was made up of a series of concentric crystal spheres, with Earth at the center, and that the motion of these spheres created a beautiful sound that human beings were incapable of hearing.

"...a cypress...my heart..." – Olivia is telling Cesario that her heart is shrouded with grief. Recall from Act II, Scene IV that the cypress tree is a symbol of mourning. The heart lies within the *bosom*, but it can also refer to the folds in a woman's clothing that cover the chest.

"methinks 'tis time to smile again" – Olivia means that she has accepted the fact that Cesario does not love her. She realizes she must stop mourning about it.

"If one should...the wolf!" – "If one should be conquered, it is better to be conquered by a noble enemy than by a cruel one."

"That you do think...you are." – Viola means that Olivia does not think that she (Olivia) is a woman in love with a woman. However, this is exactly what Olivia is (because Olivia thinks that Viola is a man).

"A murderous guilt...night is noon." – "Even the guilt of a murderer is more easily hidden than love. Love is as plain as day and is, therefore, incapable of hiding itself."

"Do not extort...unsought is better." – "Do not wrongly reason that just because I pursue you, you should not pursue me. Instead, let logic tell you this: while love that is requested is good, love that is given without being requested is even better."

<u>Act III, Scene II</u>

"like an icicle on a Dutchman's beard" – a reference to the Dutch explorer Willem Barents (1550-1597), who made three expeditions to the Arctic; on his third voyage, which took place just a few years before Shakespeare wrote *Twelfth Night*, Barents and his crew became trapped in the ice and were forced to spend the freezing winter on an island in the Arctic Ocean. Barents died on the voyage home.

"I had as lief be a Brownist as a politician." – Sir Andrew is referring to the followers of the preacher Robert Browne (1550-1633), who attacked the Church of England and advocated separation from it. Since Brownists were considered heretics, Aguecheek apparently means that he hates policy so much that he would rather be anything (even a heretic) than a politician.

"...if thou 'thou'st' him...amiss..." – The term *thou* was used when a person addressed inferiors, close friends, relatives, or children. It was very impolite to use *thou* when addressing a stranger.

"the bed of Ware in England" – The Great Bed of Ware was an impressive carved oak bed built in Ware, England, in 1590. The bed was so large it could sleep fifteen people. It is now housed in the Victoria and Albert Museum in London.

"gall enough...with a goose-pen" – Belch is punning on the word *gall*. Gall was a substance used in the making of ink. However, the word *gall* also means "bitterness" or "disagreeableness." Sir Toby makes another joke on the term *goose-pen.* A goose-pen was a quill used for writing. However, Toby uses the term to insult Andrew—the goose was symbolic of foolishness.

"I think oxen...anatomy." – The liver was thought to be the seat of courage, among other things. Sir Toby is using metaphorical language to describe Aguecheek's lack of courage.

"youngest wren of nine" – another reference to Maria's small stature; it was believed that birds usually laid nine eggs, and that the ninth would be the smallest chick.

"If you desire the spleen..." – The spleen was associated with many things, one of which was the sudden impulse to laugh.

"the new map with the augmentation of the Indies" – a reference to a new map of the world drawn in 1600 that contained additional information about the East Indies and North America

Act III, Scene III

"oft good turns...better dealing." – "Often kind actions are answered with just a 'thank-you' and nothing of more value. I wish I had money to give you that would equal the gratitude I owe you."

"the Elephant" – a reference to the name of an inn located in London during Shakespeare's time

Act III, Scene IV

"For youth is bought...borrow'd." – Olivia is admitting how desperate her infatuation with Cesario is. She is willing to buy his love with gifts if she cannot earn it the usual way.

"'Please one and please all.'" – both a popular saying at the time and the words to a particular folk ballad of the time period

"the sweet Roman hand" – Malvolio is referring to Olivia's writing. Two types of handwriting were used during the time period, the more elegant of which was the Roman style, which is similar to the handwriting we use today.

"At your request?...nightingales answer daws." – Malvolio is insulting Maria by stating that he is superior to her. He compares himself to the beautiful nightingale and Maria to the *daw* (or jackdaw), which is a crow-like bird. After questioning Maria's boldness in speaking to him, he decides that, because the superior nightingale answers the inferior daw, then it must be all right for him to answer Maria.

"midsummer madness" – It was believed at the time that the midsummer months produced insanity.

"I have limed her..." – Malvolio means that he has captured Olivia. Birdlime (or lime) was a sticky substance that was smeared on branches to trap birds.

Legion – the name Legion refers to a powerful demon, representing many demons, mentioned in the New Testament, Mark 5:9.

"Carry his water to the wise woman." – "Bring his urine to the wise woman." It was believed that certain "wise women" were able to diagnose and heal people who were cursed or possessed by demons.

"'tis not for gravity…foul collier!" – "Satan should not be playing 'cherry-pit' with such a dignified person as Malvolio. Damn the devil, that wicked coal peddler!" The term "foul collier" applies to a person who has been turned black by working with coal, and it also refers to the devil, who is usually pictured as being dark-colored. "Cherry-pit" was a children's game in which the players tried to throw cherry pits into a small hole.

"…we'll have him in a dark room and bound." – a common treatment for insanity during Shakespeare's time

cockatrices – imaginary half-rooster/half-lizard creatures that supposedly had the ability to kill with a glance

"What shall you ask…upon asking give?" – "There is nothing you can ask of me that I will deny you, as long as it does not tarnish my honor."

"He is knight…carpet consideration…" – Sir Andrew is a knight who has never used his sword in battle; he became a knight during peacetime and not during war. "Carpet consideration" means that he gained his knighthood by service to the court or through some other kind of favor.

"…on, or strip your sword…iron about you." – "Go on, or take your sword out right now, because you must fight. If you do not, you must give up your right to even carry a sword."

virago – a domineering or nagging woman; Belch is again taking advantage of Aguecheek's stupidity.

"Pox on't" – a curse; pox refers to smallpox and/or syphilis.

"Prove true…be now ta'en for you!" – Viola is expressing her hope that her brother is alive. Logically, if someone has mistaken Viola for Sebastian, it would mean that the real Sebastian has been seen somewhere.

"more a coward than a hare" – The hare (or rabbit) was believed to be a cowardly animal.

Act IV, Scene I

"after fourteen years' purchase" – Feste is implying that wise men who give their money to fools pay a high price. The value of a piece of land was usually calculated by the amount of rent collected on it during a period of twelve years. A purchase price calculated over fourteen years of rent payment would be a very high price.

"you are well fleshed" – "Well fleshed" is a hunting phrase that means "eager to fight." Hunters would give their dogs a taste of the flesh of the prey, which would whet the dog's appetite and provoke it to chase after the prey.

"He started one poor heart of mine in thee." – Olivia means that she feared for Sebastian (whom she thinks is Cesario) upon hearing Sir Toby threaten him. The statement contains a pun on the word *heart*, similar to the pun regarding the same word in the first scene of Act I. To *start* an animal is to alarm it so that it will flee into the open and become an easier target.

Lethe – In Greek mythology, Lethe was the river of forgetfulness, one of five rivers of the underworld. The others are: Acheron (sorrow), Cocytus (lamentation), Phlegethon (fire), and Styx (the river that the gods swore unbreakable oaths to).

Act IV, Scene II

"Bonos dies" – Feste is using Latin incorrectly to say "Good day."

"...the old hermit of Prague...King Gorboduc..." – The hermit of Prague is a figure most likely invented by Feste to sound like a historical figure. King Gorboduc, however, was a legendary king found in the writings of the 12th century author Geoffrey of Monmouth, whose semi-historical stories later became the source for the Arthurian legends. Feste is making fun of scholars and intellectuals by pretentiously invoking these figures. Feste continues his false intellectualism in the lines that follow.

"...thou art...Egyptians in their fog." – a reference to Old Testament (Exodus 10:22); the full quotation from the King James Version is: "And Moses stretched his hand toward heaven, and there was a thick darkness in all the land of Egypt three days."

"...this house is...dark as hell..." – Malvolio compares the darkness of his prison to the darkness of ignorance and states that ignorance itself is as dark as hell. The darkness of Malvolio's locked room is an important symbol in *Twelfth Night*. The darkness symbolizes Malvolio's supposed insanity. But, Malvolio makes it clear that the darkness symbolizes the ignorance and insanity of the rest of the household. While everyone else is busy getting drunk, playing tricks, falling in and out of love, etc., it is Malvolio who is the truly sane one. Ironically, though, he is the one who has been locked up.

Pythagoras – (570 BC-500 BC), the Greek philosopher and mathematician most famous for discovering the relationships in a triangle, which is now called the Pythagorean Theorem; the reference, however, concerns Pythagoras' belief in the transmigration of souls (more commonly known as reincarnation).

"'Hey, Robin...how thy lady does.'" – the first lines of a traditional English folk song

"five wits" – In addition to the five senses, it was believed that people had five modes of intelligence, called *wits*: common sense, imagination, fantasy, estimation (knowledge of such things as space and time), and memory.

"...the minister is here. Malvolio..." – Feste is speaking now in two voice—his own voice and the voice of Sir Topas, the priest he is pretending to be. Since Malvolio is in darkness, he does not know that Feste and Sir Topas are the same person.

"Like to the old Vice...goodman devil." – This is a reference to the morality plays popular during the 15th and 16th centuries. In a morality play, virtues, vices, and sins were embodied by actual characters. These characters would usually help the hero of the play resist the devil by threatening it with a wooden dagger.

Act IV, Scene III

"He shall conceal...to my birth." – "The priest will keep our vows secret until you are ready to make them public. We shall then have the kind of wedding celebration suitable for someone of my social position."

Act V, Scene I

"This is to give...desire my dog again." – "This is like giving a dog to someone, and in repayment for the gift, asking for it back."

"four negatives...two affirmatives" – Feste twists mathematical and grammatical logic in order to draw his conclusion that two negatives equal a positive. Note that throughout the play, Feste often makes fun of logicians and philosophers by turning logic inside out or by twisting it to absurdity.

"double-dealing" – "Double-dealing" contains two meanings in this statement: "double giving" (of the money) and "deception" or "dishonesty."

"Put your grace...flesh and blood obey it." – *Grace* contains two meanings in this statement. "Your grace" is a form of address for royalty or nobility, and the word *grace* also means "generosity."

"Primo, secundo, tertio" – [*Latin*] "first, second, third"; most likely a reference to a particular game of dice

"the third pays for all" – a proverb similar to "the third time is a charm"

Saint Bennet – shortening of Saint Benedict; probably a reference to a church called Saint Bennet Hithe, which stood near the Globe Theatre

Vulcan – the Roman god of fire and crafts; Vulcan was also the blacksmith of the gods and was believed to be the source of volcanoes.

"With which such scathful...honour on him." – "He fought and conquered our best ship with such fierce determination that we could not help but admire him."

"Candy" – [*slang*] *Candia*, which referred to the islands in and around the island of Crete off the coast of Greece

"And grew a twenty years...one would wink..." – "And, in the blink of an eye, acted as if we were as distant as we would be if twenty years had come between us."

"the Egyptian thief" – a reference to the *Aethiopica*, a romance by the third century Greek writer Heliodorus of Emesa; the ancient story was discovered and printed in the 16th century. The allusion is to the character of Thyamis, who was in love with Chariclea. When his life was in danger, Thyamis plotted to kill Chariclea so that no other man could have her upon his death.

"Be that thou know'st…as that thou fear'st." – Olivia is telling Cesario to stop hiding the fact that he has vowed to marry her. She begs him to accept his identity as her fiancé and the fact that he is now as noble as Duke Orsino. Remember, however, that it is really Sebastian with whom Olivia has exchanged a vow, not Cesario, as Olivia believes.

"Or will not else thy craft…thine overthrow?" – "Or will you get so deeply into your tricks that you'll make a mistake and be destroyed by them?"

"a passy-measure, or a pavin" – "Passy-measure" is Sir Toby's way of corrupting the Italian word *passamezzo*, which is the name of a particular slow dance. *Pavin* refers to a slow, somber Spanish dance. While it is not entirely clear what Sir Toby means to say, it is obvious that he means to insult the doctor. He might be likening the doctor's slowness to the slowness of the dances.

Messaline – the fictional home country of Sebastian and Viola

Vox – [*Latin*] *voice*; Feste is telling Olivia that she must let him read the letter out loud in his imitation of a madman's voice.

"To think me as well a sister as a wife" – Olivia means a *sister-in-law*. When Olivia marries Sebastian, she will become Viola's sister-in-law. Then, when Viola marries Orsino, Olivia will become Orsino's sister-in-law through marriage.

"He hath not told us of the captain yet…" – The *captain* is the sea captain who rescued Viola and who is in possession of her female clothing. He is still in prison due to a lawsuit which Malvolio brought against him. This fact and Feste's sad song at the close of the play, add a disquieting note to the otherwise lightheartedness of the story. This is because the couples have agreed to wait for the sea captain's proof before they allow the weddings to take place.

"Cesario, come…his fancy's queen." – It is interesting that Orsino still calls Viola by the name of Cesario. This seems to support an underlying theme regarding clothing and identity. Throughout the play, characters use clothing to disguise their identity. Feste wears a priest's clothing to impersonate Sir Topas; Malvolio changes his attire to impress Olivia; Viola dresses like a young man in order to hide her own identity. It seems that identity is an almost fluid concept for the characters, as it is constantly shifting. Even though Orsino now knows Viola's true identity, he is still able to see her as the boy he thought she was.

"For the rain it raineth every day." – The song is a sad and serious one about the harshness of life. After all the merriness and confusion of *Twelfth Night*, Feste's song makes for a bittersweet ending to the play, perhaps reminding us that not all endings are entirely happy ones.

Vocabulary

Act I, Scene I

abatement – a lessening
cloistress – a nun
fantastical – unreal, fanciful
handmaid – a female attendant
hart – a male deer
pestilence – disease
surfeiting – filling to excess

Act I, Scene II

abjured – renounced; gave up
bounteously – plentifully, abundantly
prattle – mindless chatter
provident – wise

Act I, Scene III

allay – to calm; to put to rest
barren – empty
bestowed – granted, gave
distaff – a rod that holds flax or other fiber during spinning
flax – a type of fiber used in making textiles
forswear – to renounce; to give up
prodigal – wasteful; reckless
prudent – sensible, practical
quaffing – drinking, guzzling
revels – parties
shrew – a scolding woman

Act I, Scene IV

aloof – detached, distant
belie – to contradict or disprove
clamorous – noisy, boisterous
discourse – talk, discussion
gait – a manner of walking
inconstant – changeable
negligence – carelessness, neglect

Act I, Scene V

amend – to improve; to alter
assurance – a guarantee or promise

blazon – a coat of arms
cuckold – a man whose wife has cheated on him
decreed – ruled, commanded, ordered
dexteriously – [dexterously] skillfully, expertly
disposition – temperament, nature
distempered – diseased
feigned – pretended, faked
fertile – abundant, bountiful
fervor – a passion for
heresy – sacrilege; profane or unorthodox opinion
homage – respect, reverence, worship
infirmity – ill-health; also, weakness due to aging (in Shakespeare's time)
lethargy – laziness; stupor
misprision – a mistake, error
mollification – appeasement; the act or state of being calmed down
nonpareil – without equal
overture – a proposal or suggestion
parentage – ancestry, origin
peevish – irritable, bad-tempered
resolute – firm, unyielding
reverberate – to echo
rogue – a scoundrel
sustain – to suffer; to incur
syllogism – a type of logical argument
transgresses – lapses; goes astray
usurp – to take over; seize without the right to do so
valiant – brave, courageous
yond – over there

Act II, Scene I
determinate – decisive
extort – to extract or obtain in a forceful manner
malignancy – malevolence, wickedness

Act II, Scene II
churlish – rude, impolite
frailty – weakness
thriftless – unprofitable

Act II, Scene III
caterwauling – loud shrieking; unpleasant noise making
constrained – obliged, compelled

disposed – willing, inclined
epistles – letters
equinoctial – referring to the line that marks the midway point between the northern and southern poles
indignation – righteous anger
knave – a rogue or villain
mellifluous – smoothly flowing
mitigation – alleviation; lessening of intensity or severity

Act II, Scene IV

damask – a blend of red and white
opal – a type of gem
pined – sulked, brooded
retention – the ability to keep or hold
spinsters – women who worked at spinning yarn
wavering – indecisive, fickle

Act II, Scene V

abhors – hates
austere – strict, severe
commend – to praise; compliment
demure – modest
detests – hates
dowry – a gift of money or property from a bride's family to the husband
exult – to gloat; rejoice
injunction – a command or order
manifests – reveals; makes known
mockery – ridicule, derision
niggardly – stingy, ungenerous
pension – an income, allowance
portend – to foretell; signify
prerogative – a privilege, right
quenching – stifling, extinguishing
sinews – muscles, tendons
surly – rude, gruff

Act III, Scene I

construe – to interpret
courtier – an aristocrat
desirous – eager
fetter – to tie or bind
whet – to stimulate or awaken; sharpen

Act III, Scene II

augmentation – an addition, extension
exasperate – to frustrate or annoy
laudable – praiseworthy, admirable
prevail – to triumph or succeed

Act III, Scene III

unhospitable – unwelcoming, unfriendly

Act III, Scene IV

adheres – sticks to, holds tightly
coffer – money
concurs – agrees
couplet – two rhymed lines of poetry
devout – religious, devoted
dram – a unit of measurement; small amount
entreat – to beg
headstrong – willful, stubborn
impetuosity – impulsiveness, rashness
implacable – stubborn; unyielding
incites – provokes, rouses
intercepter – one who interrupts the progress of someone or something
pacified – calmed, placated
paltry – wretched, miserable
penance – an act of self-punishment
perdition – destruction, ruin
prospect – an expectation
rapier – a double-edged sword
rave – to rant; talk deliriously
reproof – criticism, blame
sanctity – holiness, purity
scabbard – a sheath for a sword
swaggering – overconfident, arrogant
venerable – honored, respected
vile – wicked, low
wrath – anger

Act IV, Scene I

barbarous – brutal, uncivilized
ruffian – a hooligan
tarry – to delay or linger

wretch – a miserable person

Act IV, Scene II

convey – to communicate; to express
curate – a cleric, pastor
dispossess – to deprive; to strip
notoriously – infamously, disgracefully

Act IV, Scene III

consecrated – holy, sacred

Act V, Scene I

adverse – hostile
bounty – a payment, reward
cohere – to join together
contrary – opposite
covetousness – greed
deity – a god
edified – instructed, enlightened
induced – provoked, caused
interim – an interval
peruse – to read carefully
plaintiff – the accuser or claimant in a lawsuit
reverence – respect, admiration